REUNION

A Search for Ancestors

CHAPTER 1

EMBERS

Of all the big questions, "Where do I come from?" is the most elusive. To answer it, you have to go looking for what's no longer visible, and listen for what can no longer talk back.

And what do you have to go on? A fossil, maybe, or messages written in a lost language. Coffin air where there used to be breath.

But go back to some place where you used to live, some place you come from, and things have a sneaky way of reigniting. This house, this street no longer feels like home, and so you can't help but see it through the eyes you had when it *was* home: This restaurant wasn't here, but the house over there looks just the same, and the view down the street almost does, too, and this floor creaks with the same feet.

The old haunt is starting to haunt.

This is when you might notice little eruptions of how you felt back then, and how you saw things, and who you were, and who you were with. You might hear some sayings of the gone, or feel the scratch of discarded skin. Comfort zones have somehow stayed in you, traces of an old belonging, so that Robert Graves' lines about the dead could also be said of past homes: "Blow on a dead man's embers / And a live flame will start."

For some of us, the embers of a place might stay burning even if we've never been there. To an American, say, whose parents immigrated from elsewhere, this *elsewhere* has always been everywhere—in the language and accents she heard around the house as she was growing up, the stories she was told, the habits she was taught. Her family's homeland isn't so much a place as it is a part of her, something she couldn't disentangle from herself even if she wanted to, and if she happens to visit where her parents grew up, it's not as a stranger, but almost as a native returning from a long absence. The country of her ancestors carries the allure of home, the almost proven promise of home, no matter where she goes.

Even for her, though, the ancestral homeland isn't quite home. Korean-American, Polish-American, Mexican-American: Those hyphens suggest to the world that she's not *fully* Korean, not *completely* Polish, not *wholly* Mexican. Her belonging to that place isn't immediate, as it was for her parents. For her, it's at the slightest remove.

And for someone like me, the remove isn't even slight. Growing up in Chatham, Illinois, my family's origins were almost invisible. No stories of voyages had been passed down, no customs or memories had been brought over to be kept simmering.

Sure, I looked at the names of my grandparents and great-grandparents, and so I could imagine Ireland or Germany or England, but those places were far off. They were just words. There wasn't much of an *elsewhere* in the background—history seemed to start in about 1776. It was as if my family had sprung out of the ground in America, grilling burgers and going bowling.

My mom's mom, Betty McDonald, liked it that way. If the Census Bureau had come to the door and asked for her ethnic origin, she would have responded with one word: America. She would have said: Why does it matter? You are who you are, you should be judged on that, it doesn't matter whether your parents came from Pennsylvania or Italy or Eskimo land, or wherever the heck it was. Are people who lived two hundred years ago going to put food on your table? Are they going to give you an education? For all you know, your great-great-whatever was a real son of a gun, so now are you going to take credit for that, too?

Grandma knew the nice old ladies who didn't mind letting everybody know that their ancestors came over on the Mayflower, and served in the Revolutionary War. I can see the look she would have given the Mayflower ladies. It said: You don't fool me. Don't act as if you deserve some special honor just by breathing—I know the truth, and you know the truth, so let's be honest here.

All right then, the truth is that I can't think of home without thinking of her. Her voice reading to me for hours when I was too sick to go to school, and her applause at the end of every performance I put on for her, even though I was just running around and acting like Batman. The opening sounds of *M.A.S.H.*, her favorite show, when I ran in from outside, and how she always asked me if I wanted to watch it with her.

Her laugh-out-loud laugh, her wry and sly jokes.

As a girl, she always wanted to run track, but school officials wouldn't let her be in any of the meets. She decided to practice after school with the boys anyway, and years later, when my mom wanted to play softball and Grandma found out there was no girls' team in Chatham, she decided to start one, and served as a coach right alongside Grandpa. Ryan, she'd tell me, if it's what you want to do, and you know it's right, then you just go ahead and do it, and don't let them tell you any different, because they don't know. Just keep plugging along and do your best, and don't make a fuss, now, don't make some big production out of it.

The last time she went to the hospital, I was away from home, about to finish my second year of college. Those first few semesters had been tough, and I hadn't done as well as I'd hoped. She called to say she'd have to go in for an operation, but everything was going to be fine and I shouldn't worry. She told me I should just push ahead and study hard and do as well as I could on my finals, and she was rooting for me. Only later did I find out that things weren't as good as she'd let on. Only later did I find out that she'd decided to take the risk of heart surgery despite her weak lungs.

So when I came back home a few days after my last exam, and found Mom and everyone else waiting for me, it didn't matter that my grades had arrived in the mail earlier that day. And as I walked into the hospital room and saw the respirator and the tubes, Mom told me that Grandma's eyes were closed and she couldn't speak, but she could still hear us, and she was able to write out whole sentences on a note pad.

I took her hand. Hi Grandma, it's Ryan. She squeezed my hand back. I looked over at the machine that beeped each heartbeat. I wanted to tell her: You didn't have to do what you did for me, I could have come home earlier, I could have figured out a way to take my exams later on. The breathing machine made its sucking, in-and-out sound. I wanted to say: I've never understood how I deserved what you did for me all those times. But there were people around, and so I just said: Well, my grades came in, and it turns out I made it onto the Dean's List. She motioned for the note pad, and I handed her a pen. She wrote: As long as it isn't a hit list.

Even now, she can prick bubbles—her voice is the one I hear whenever I find myself dismissing people who've let their fantasies get the best of them. Her voice is the one I hear when I press the mute button as the commercials come on.

And her you-don't-fool-me look is what comes to mind when I hear someone say that the land of his ancestors is like home. Right. Never mind that paying a fare and visiting for a while aren't enough to make you belong there, not just yet, because it takes years of everyday seeing and breathing to be woven into a place.

Still, the pre-cooked homeland nostalgia is all around. There are the Chinese New Year parades, the restaurants with names like Socrates Diner, the lederhosen and wheat beer in the old German neighborhoods. Perhaps the most finely tuned nostalgia industry is the Celtic one—look no further than the local Irish Pub, showing off its authenticity with copies of old Guinness advertisements, a framed Irish Blessing, maybe a photo of John F. Kennedy. If you don't act now, you might even pass up the chance to have your very own tartan bagpiper Santa Claus ornament, and *Braveheart* just might explain why you're fiercely independent and loyal.

But when people visit the land of their ancestors, many of them find something more *real* than the ad campaigns, something they can't put into words. They come away sensing a tug that surprises even them. Afterwards, they say: It was like some part of me belonged there. Or: Every once in a while, I got this weird feeling that I knew the place already.

When they talk about the trip, you can hear them saying one thing that they never fully spell out. It's that the country they live in, no matter how close they are to it, and no matter how devoted they are to it, can't answer every question they want it to. A part of them needs more than what their country can give. Something older, something beyond "the New World."

Most people living in this New World have been chasing the immediate for a long while now, and many of us have the creeping suspicion that after all this time, something is missing. Whole cities grow up in a decade or two, and people move wherever circumstances take them. The brand new houses sprout up to the horizon, accompanied by the same new gas stations with the same new chain restaurants. I'm expected to reinvent myself, as if who I am is just an outfit than I can step in and out of. The constant churn has come to be our norm—the shunting of tradition has become our tradition.

The thing is, we're the exception. For thousands of years, most people have seen themselves, not as the creators of their own lives, but as carriers of a tradition, the tradition that made them who they were. Many people throughout the world still think of themselves in the same way, as swatches of a very old fabric, without the clean break of mass migrations, and forced forgettings, and declarations of independence. We might be the first culture powered by the assumption that we can be satisfied by the ever-new, with only a few flashes of something older and encompassing.

Maybe that's why a lot of us can no longer deny the old need for groundedness, the need to see that our home and our origin might be the same. Maybe that's why, in the years after Grandma left, I'd go into a bookstore and find a book with a title like *Clans and Tartans*. I'd read through the names: Douglas, MacDougall, Gordon, Grant, Robertson. For each one, there'd be a short history, along with the clan's motto and tartan. Sometimes there'd be images of warriors, wearing their tartan kilts and playing their bagpipes and drawing their swords, ready to fight the English or a rival clan. In some books, I could find a map of the Scottish Highlands that outlined clan origins by pinning names to particular places.

When I looked for Grandma's maiden name, I was never disappointed. My family spelled it "McDonald" rather than "MacDonald," but apparently there was no difference, and so I belonged to Clan Donald—one of the oldest and most powerful clans, according to the guidebooks. By the 15th century, the MacDonalds controlled much of the Highlands and the islands of the Hebrides. The clan was large enough to have several different branches, each with its own tartan, each with its own chief: MacDonald of Sleat, of Glengarry, of

Ardnamurchan and others.

As I got into the history and legends, though, I knew not to take them too personally: I could only trace my McDonald family back to Missouri. What if my ancestors had come from Ireland rather than Scotland? What if one of my ancestors had been adopted by an unrelated family named McDonald? I knew that the name meant "son of Donald" in Scottish Gaelic, so maybe I just had an ancestor with a father named Donald. Maybe, somewhere along the line, there'd been what genealogists gently call a "non-paternity event."

But those unknowns only made me want to know more. The drawing of the curtains only made me want to see who was behind them. These people, unnamed, faceless, were hiding out of view, right beyond the beginning of the dark. Just who *were* my ancestors?

And with that question, a journey started. A journey that would lead to country graveyards, faded names in old books, and a DNA shock. A journey that would uncover a story of rebellion and survival, and would take me to one ancient place, far away, where I'd find embers burning for me even after all these years.

CHAPTER 2

BEGINNING
HINTS

The first step should have been easy—ask people what they knew about my recent McDonald family. But Grandma never knew much about them, and neither did her dad, my great-grandpa Lee McDonald. My mom and Aunt Donna asked him the question several times, and his response was always the same.

"Where did your family come from, Grandpa?"

"Missouri."

"No, we mean before then. Where did they come from originally?"

"Kentucky."

It's not that he had any reason to be ashamed of his family's past, as far as we knew. He just didn't consider family origins to be important.

And maybe he had a point.

Just think of a photograph: Nineteenth century, a man and a woman, two of your ancestors. No crinkled eyes or fixed smiles here, no lips saying cheese. He's wearing a dark suit and tie, and she's wearing a black or gray dress that goes all the way to her ankles, with a collar that buttons tightly around her neck. Their arms are folded on their laps.

And when you focus on their eyes, you won't see much, because the picture blurs when you zero in. You can't quite see the white around her pupils, or the eye wrinkles he must have had from hours in the sun. You can't see in their eyes what you see in a friend who trades a knowing glance with you, because these ancestors never had the chance to know you, and so they never spoke of you, they never cared about you. What would they have thought of you if they were around today? Would they invite you in, like you were some long lost grandchild of theirs, or would they be polite and distant, the way they might treat a strange new acquaintance?

Each of us could ask these questions, but we know that there can be no response. We were never given the chance to know all the ways he would look after us, or how she would smile at us, or how they might have spoken of us, even when it was just the two of them. Our ancestors are never going to return our calls.

But, spookily, they're here. Their DNA is *our* DNA, in us right now, influencing everything our bodies and minds do. We might maintain their traditions. We might pledge allegiance to their flags. Maybe our virtues and our fears are only variations on theirs, written in a different key. Our ancestors populate a no man's land in us: They're gone but not gone, here but not here, residing somewhere between absence and presence.

At least I had one foothold: I knew who my great-grandpa Lee McDonald's parents were. Their names were William

McDonald and Melinda Hagan, and they went by Will and Linnie. My great-grandpa Lee was born in a small town north of St. Louis, but when he was a boy, his parents Will and Linnie moved the family to Chatham, Illinois, my hometown, in the middle of the state. Mom and Aunt Donna and Uncle Del remembered Will's dry sense of humor and his stoic quiet, and Linnie's unassuming sweetness. But their history back in Missouri was a mystery.

And there were so many chances for us to try to find out, because when I was growing up in Chatham, my great-grandpa Lee and his wife, my great-grandma Mary, were always around—they'd come over to our house for lunch or dinner, and they were at most of their great-grandchildren's birthday parties, sporting events, dance recitals. The two of them would sit together at the table after a Sunday dinner, and he'd be telling a funny story, and she'd play along. Everybody always said that if you wanted to find Great-grandpa, you should look for Great-grandma, and there he'd be.

By the time I got to know her, though, she wasn't able to be what she was before. Yes, in this picture, where the two of them are holding up a cake reading "Happy 49th Anniversary Mom & Dad," there's no sign on her face of any change on the horizon. But within a few years after that picture was taken, gradually, more and more, he'd have to remember for her. If she were wearing long sleeves that day, he'd roll them up before giving her the shots she needed.

After a while, whenever she made it out of the house, it was only because he took her around in the wheelchair. Now Mary, we're gonna go see David play baseball, you remember

David, your granddaughter Linda's son. Toward the end, in the nursing home, and then in the hospital, he'd ask her to open her mouth, and eat some of this food, because it's good for you, and you need it.

Even after that, even after he lost her, he had a lot of people to take care of, as a grandpa does. After my baseball games, he'd take me over to the ice cream place by the elementary school and buy me a chocolate and vanilla swirled ice cream cone. There was the time he took me to the optometrist because I wanted a new pair of glasses, the time he taught me how to put the worm on the hook.

And there was his grin. It wasn't the self-conscious kind: It would come up from inside him whenever the occasion for a smile arose, which for him was most of the time.

That smile might surprise anyone who knew where he came from. As a child, he had to live with another family for a while because there wasn't enough for him and his brothers and sisters, and he had to quit school after 8th grade to work in a coalmine. Even when he was a young man, his children would wake up on Christmas morning to find that their only gifts were ripe oranges, one for each of them, placed in their stockings. But he always knew he was lucky, because he had a love that never went away, and the assurance that he never left his beliefs, and some chances to pass down what matters, and a lot of graduations.

He was here for so long that he passed away just a year before his daughter, my grandma. After the two of them were gone, I still respected their suspicions, their boredom with the dead. But now I'd seen *Braveheart*, and I'd learned from those *Clans and Tartans* books. And now I'd found an accomplice—my mom. We began entertaining the suspicion that we were MacDonalds, despite that little hang-up about our family records only going back to the late 1800s.

We decided to try out the Scottish Highland revival.

We made our way to the Highland Games in Springfield, Illinois, where we listened to the bagpipers and watched big guys in kilts do the caber toss and the Scottish hammer throw. We watched the girls do Highland dancing. We went up to the Clan Donald tent and picked up a pamphlet without letting on just who we were. A guy said something in Gaelic over the loudspeaker, and nobody knew what it meant, but it was a big hit anyway. Mom bought a bumper sticker that read, "Have you hugged a Scot today?" Beer was involved, which might explain why my memories are hazy, but I remember that I found a miniature British flag to buy, just for fun, and the man selling it called it "the limey."

Because just as David needed Goliath, just as Luke Skywalker needed the Dark Side of the Force, a pro-Celtic movement has to be anti-English. The Englishman will never win at this game: He's either an aristocratic snob, or a jackass who beats up people at soccer matches. He's either a polite wimp, or is always aiming to prey and conquer. He's everything that the Celt isn't—cold and stale rather than warm and creative, intellectual rather than vital, pompous rather than down-to-earth, backstabber rather than straight shooter.

But it's not enough, at the Highland Games in Springfield, Illinois, to content ourselves with anti-English jabs. No, we also have our clan rivalries to be responsible for. Later in the day, a man named Campbell got up to do the caber toss, and—again, just for fun—I booed. I did it softly enough that Mr. Campbell couldn't hear me, but loudly enough that the couple standing next to me could. They gave me a knowing look and asked which clan I was from. When I gave the answer, they replied, "Ah yes, we know all about the MacDonalds and the Campbells."

It was the most famous bad blood in Scottish history. The two clans were enemies for centuries, fighting for control of much of the Highlands. By now, the details of this civil war have mostly been forgotten, replaced by a vague sense of distrust, even among those who take it seriously. For others, it's so far back in the past that the only reason worth mentioning it is to get an easy laugh. *The Economist*, in a book review, showed a hamburger fighting a can of soup.

One event, though, is still remembered, and has come to crystallize the MacDonald-Campbell grudge in the minds of many people: In February 1692, in what's become known as the "Massacre of Glencoe," British government troops under the command of a Robert Campbell fell upon the people of Glencoe, the smallest branch of the MacDonalds. The troops had arrived in Glencoe about two weeks earlier, and the MacDonalds had taken them in, giving them all hospitality—shelter, food and drink. Men, women and children were slaughtered in the middle of the night or froze to death as they tried to escape. A song by Jim McLean tells the story:

They came in a blizzard, we offered them heat,
A roof o'er their heads, dry shoes for their feet,

We wined them and dined them, they ate of our meat,
And they slept in the house of MacDonald.

Oh, cruel is the snow that sweeps Glencoe
And covers the grave o' Donald,
Oh, cruel was the foe that raped Glencoe
And murdered the house of MacDonald.

Most of the troops weren't Campbells, and the orders came from the British king and his Scottish officials rather than a Campbell chief, but it's mostly come to be seen as a massacre of "the MacDonalds" by "the Campbells." At the reception desk at the Clachaig Inn, a bed and breakfast in Glencoe, there's a sign that reads: "No hawkers or Campbells."

As evening approached, Mom and I left the Highland Games with our bumper sticker, our miniature flag, and a new CD of bagpipe music. And from time to time over the next few years, those bagpipes would fill up my apartment, and websites would show me tartan kilts and tell Gaelic legends.

Still, the Highlands were hypothetical, because my McDonald family tree could only say this:

Will McDonald (1875-1964), m. Linnie Hagan
|
Lee McDonald (my great-grandpa), m. Mary Bridgewater
|
Betty McDonald (my grandma), m. Don McCord

Then, one weekend, Mom and Aunt Donna were going through some boxes that had been at Great-grandpa Lee's house. When they opened one of the boxes, they saw black and white pictures and old newspaper cut outs, wedged in next to each other, stacked on top of one another.

Here was Grandma as a girl, smiling with Shirley Temple curls, sitting at her desk like the other kids, and her teacher was standing erect in the back, with the cursive on the blackboards all around, and a profile of George Washington hung on the wall. Here was Great-grandpa Lee as a young man, standing in front of the little church where his parents had gotten married. Here was a cutout from the *Chatham Clarion*: "Mr. and Mrs. William H. McDonald of Chatham will mark their 60th wedding anniversary Thursday. They have lived in Chatham for 43 years and are the parents of eight children, all living. They also have 14 grandchildren and 14 great-grandchildren."

And down in that box, tucked in with the photos and newspaper clippings, someone had left a white envelope. Mom and Aunt Donna pulled it out. There was no writing on the envelope—no names, no scribbles, no return address.

But inside it was a letter.

CHAPTER 3

OL' SCOTTY

The handwriting was unknown, and the letter was unsigned, but it listed Will and Linnie and their birth dates and death dates, and it said that Linnie's parents were Thomas and Lucy Hagan. And there, at the top, it said that Will's parents were William Duncan McDonald (1855-1935) and Georgianna "Anna" Wilson (1854-1920). Then it said that Georgianna Wilson's father was William Wilson, and that William Duncan McDonald's parents were Hiram McDonald and Nancy Buchanan.

Mom knew I was coming home in a few weeks for Christmas, so she waited to show me the letter. I'd graduated from law school a year before, and I was working as a lawyer in New York. This was the first time my girlfriend Penny, a New Yorker, was coming back to Chatham to meet the family. We had all the introductions, and then the we-really-like-her, and the I-really-like-them.

It was at the end of the trip when Mom sat with Penny and me and showed us the old letter. When I first saw it, I said "William Duncan McDonald" and "Georgianna Wilson" silently to myself, as if I'd just been introduced to them and wanted to make sure not to forget their names. Since I'd never known anything about them, they'd been these mystery placeholders on the family tree. Now, with their names and a few dates, they somehow seemed more real to me.

So my McDonald family tree suddenly looked like this:

Hiram McDonald, m. Nancy Buchanan
|
William Duncan McDonald (1855-1935), m. Georgianna Wilson
|
Will McDonald (1875-1964), m. Linnie Hagan
|
Lee McDonald (my great-grandpa), m. Mary Bridgewater
|
Betty McDonald (my grandma), m. Don McCord

But who were the parents of Hiram McDonald? I started with the serious researcher's most time-tested method—the Google search. I found several Hiram McDonalds, but none of them could have been *my* Hiram, based on their dates, where they lived and whom they married.

Still, I knew that Great-grandpa Lee's family was from Missouri, and I wondered whether any Missouri records were online. At Ancestry.com, I typed in my great-great-great-great-grandma Nancy Buchanan's name, and within a few seconds, I was looking at a page showing that she married Hiram McDonald on April 7, 1836 in Lincoln County.

I was surprised to find out that Hiram and Nancy were in Missouri that early. But I wasn't surprised to find that Lincoln County is just south of Pike County, where their great-grandson, my great-grandpa Lee, was born.

Then I saw that census records were available, too, and they could be searched by name. Somehow, I trusted whoever had written that letter sitting at the bottom of the box, but these census entries might be able to confirm what the letter said—or maybe tell a different story altogether.

I started with the 1900 census; I knew for sure that Will and Linnie were Great-grandpa Lee's parents, and I knew they'd gotten married in 1898, so the 1900 census would be the first one that would list them together as a household. I typed in Will's name, and in an instant I was looking at an image of the original census page, ink smudges and all. There they were, about halfway down the page: William and Linnie McDonald, living in Pike County.

And just two doors down were William McDonald, born in August 1855, and Annie McDonald, born in November 1854. The names and dates matched up with what the letter said about Will's parents, William Duncan McDonald and Georgianna "Anna" Wilson. That's what you'd expect of a young couple, just starting out—they'd be living next to family.

I went back ten years, but found out that most of the 1890 census records had been destroyed by fire. So I went further back, to 1880, and there I found William and Georgia McDonald in Pike County, both aged twenty-five, with a young son named William. This proved the letter right: Will, the little boy in 1880, was the son of William and Georgianna McDonald.

Then, another ten years back, in the 1870 census, I found

a fifteen-year-old named Duncan McDonald in Lincoln County. This had to be my William Duncan, born in 1855. The names of his parents? Hiram and Nancy McDonald.

So the census records proved what Mom and Aunt Donna found in that box: My great-great-grandpa Will really was the son of William Duncan and Georgianna, and William Duncan really was the son of Hiram and Nancy. Now that I thought about it, I could have uncovered these things all along, just through census records.

But would those records reveal Hiram's parents?

I knew that Hiram was in Lincoln County by 1836, when he married Nancy and the two of them started a household. I hoped that I could find his parents by finding Hiram listed in *their* household in the pre-1840 censuses, but it turned out that in those censuses, the census takers only asked for the name of the head of the household, so Hiram couldn't be found there.

The online 1850-1880 censuses, though, asked people which state or country they were born in. By knowing where Hiram was born, I'd at least be able to narrow the search for his parents to one state or country—maybe Scotland or Ireland.

I looked, and noticed something strange: In 1850, Hiram told the census taker that he'd been born in Kentucky, but in the 1860, 1870 and 1880 censuses, he said Ohio. Had there been some Ohio-Kentucky border dispute I was unaware of? Or had someone else in the household talked to the census taker, giving the wrong answer for some reason?

Fortunately, the 1880 census asked people where their

parents had been born, and here Hiram (or someone else) said that his parents had been born in Kentucky. But from the census records, I knew that Hiram was born in about 1807, so his parents were probably born before the end of the Revolutionary War—probably too early to have been in Kentucky or Ohio already.

Then I noticed something even stranger: In the 1860, 1870 and 1880 censuses, the family name was given as Mc-Donald, but in the 1850 census, it was McDaniel. Soon I found a family tree at Rootsweb.com that mentioned Hiram and Nancy's daughter Mary, calling her Mary McDaniel, and giving Hiram's last name as MackDaniel. Did Hiram change his name from McDaniel to McDonald? Had my family been McDaniels all this time, without knowing it?

I'd heard of immigrants changing their names upon arriving in America, and I had no reason to think that the same thing couldn't have happened in 19th century Missouri. According to some websites, the name McDaniel was simply another version of the Scottish name McDonald, but according to *The Dictionary of American Family Names*, McDaniel was a version of the Irish name McDonnell.

The more I searched, the less I knew.

Maybe other people out there had their own family records that mentioned Hiram. But how could I get in contact with them, if they even existed? I typed "Lincoln County Missouri genealogy" into Google and found the Lincoln County GenWeb site, part of the US GenWeb Project. It seemed to have everything you might need if you had Lincoln County ancestors—a message board, old maps, tips on how to find marriages and deaths and burials. And here was a Surname Registry, where anyone interested in a particular family could leave their name and email address. Under "McDonald," I found a man named Ray Bell.

I decided to give it a shot. I emailed him what I knew about Hiram, and a few days later I got a response. His Mc-Donalds/McDaniels weren't related to mine, but he'd learned a little about Hiram, and had kept some notes just in case. He didn't know who Hiram's parents were, but he knew Hiram had a brother named Thomas, who married Nancy Presley in Lincoln County in 1839.

Now that I knew a little more, I felt comfortable posting a query about Hiram and his brother Thomas on Internet message boards, and I waited again. Within a day, I got a response. A man named Dennis Korinek told me that he was descended from Nancy Presley, not through her marriage to Thomas, but through her second marriage.

Dennis didn't know anything about Hiram and Thomas' parents, but at least his family had passed down some sense of what Thomas was like. According to a letter written by Thomas' great-grandson, "'Scotty' McDonald was hunted by the law from one end of Missouri to the other. My mother told me once that her mother, Naomi, told her that once a posse almost caught McDonald. But he escaped by running outside and jumping into a horse trough, leaving only his nose sticking out of the water so he could breathe. This happened at night, and the posse searched the house and barn. But never thought of looking in the horse trough."

When I told Mom about ol' Scotty, she was quiet for a

second and then said, "You know, that's funny, I just remembered that Grandpa used to talk about how people in his family would run around with Jesse James." As soon as she said that, I remembered that Great-grandpa Lee had told me the same thing when I was a little boy. Even though he didn't think family history mattered much, that rule apparently didn't apply to the part about cavorting with famous killers.

And now I could imagine getting an email that revealed Hiram's origins, because if one perfect stranger knew a family story about a posse and a horse trough, then there just had to be another who knew an older story.

While I waited, I tried one new thing. I'd already searched for Hiram and Nancy on Ancestry.com and Google, but maybe there was some record out there that gave their surname without listing their first names. Soon I found myself back at the Lincoln County GenWeb site, where I saw this transcription of a gravestone at the Bryant Creek Cemetery:

H. McDONALD - b: Nov. 12, 1806; d: Oct. 17, 1882
M. McDONALD - b: Dec. 16, 1818; d: July 17, 1910

The letter M in this "M. McDonald" almost made me click away, but then I saw that these people had to be Hiram and Nancy. The 1900 census had asked for the month and year of a person's birth, and in that census Nancy had said December 1818. The transcriber of this gravestone had simply mistaken an N for an M.

So now I knew exactly when Hiram and Nancy were born, and exactly when they died. Their gravestone also showed that they went by McDonald, not McDaniel, so if my ancestors had once been McDaniels, the switch happened prior to Hiram.

All right then. If there were some record, somewhere, that referenced a Hiram McDonald/McDaniel who was born on November 12, 1806 and died on October 17, 1882, then I'd know that this was *my* Hiram, and that might lead me to his family.

It *might*. And over the next few months, I got used to that *might*. Someone might email me to say who Hiram's parents were. A new search on Google or Ancestry.com or Familysearch.org might reveal a new clue. I'd known from the beginning that this would probably take time, and I'd never expected it to be easy, but I'd hoped to uncover my McDonald ancestors before the upcoming family trip.

To Scotland.

Penny and I were getting married, and we'd settled on a church outside of Edinburgh, with a honeymoon up in the Highlands. Rather than have a big wedding in New York or Chatham, we'd decided to, ahem, channel our resources in a different way—keep things small, and far off. Since none of our family or friends had been to Scotland, the escape would be part of the experience.

Although no one from my dad's side of the family would be able to make it, most of my mom's family would be there, and they were getting ready, thinking about the places they'd see. There were whispers of kilt buying and rumors of haggis eating. I still wasn't sure about our supposed connection to Clan Donald, but I'd been overruled; all the men in the family would be wearing MacDonald tartan ties on the big day, except those of us in the wedding party. Peggy, Grandma's little sister, would be wearing a MacDonald tartan sash.

As Penny and I boarded the plane, our carry-on luggage was a long, white dress. People around us gave smiling glances, and a few congratulations, as a flight attendant found a closet to hang the dress in. We buckled our seatbelts and checked our phones to make sure there weren't any more emails to worry about. The groomsmen's suits were ready to be picked up, and the bridesmaids knew when to show up at Angus Gordon Hairdressing, and the bagpiper knew which songs to play. Our bed-and-breakfasts in the Highlands were all booked.

The plane started moving, then turned. It slowed down for a few seconds, and then picked up speed again and headed down the runway. I knew I had no right to expect that everyone would be able to make it to Scotland for this, but I was just wishing we could have had that one moment, when I see the two of them grin at each other right before I say: Grandma, this is Penny, and Penny, this is my grandma.

CHAPTER 4

THE CHURCH,
ON TIME

In Edinburgh, the gray stones aren't just in the houses, but in the streets, too, and the buildings date from the Middle Ages to the 18th century. The roads are narrow and a little hilly, and so they turn and wind around. Every time you glance up, there's the medieval Edinburgh Castle, built into the hollow of an extinct volcano that looms over everything, distant in the air, always looking down at you. It was early July, with flowers at almost every address, bright reds and blues and yellows up against stone.

Penny and I were on our way to a pub, where we were going to meet up with my family before dinner. We spotted the pub from across the street, and as we walked toward it, smiling Americans came out to give us a welcome hug. Here were Grandma and Grandpa's three children—Mom, Aunt Donna and Uncle Del—along with their spouses and children. And here was Grandma's younger sister, Peggy, with her husband Dave and son Jay.

The next thing I knew, there was a beer in front of me, and Penny and I were hearing about some of the things we'd missed so far—the explorations around the city, the coziness of their apartments, how warmly and politely people had treated them. Mom told me about hikes all over town, hikes that happened despite hunger and tired legs, because you can't let yourself miss anything.

The next day was for last-minute errands and little expeditions around the city. Listening to traditional Irish and Scottish music at a pub that night, I was relieved that this first full day had been low-key, because tomorrow looked to be lively: We'd have the protests to contend with.

That's right, the protests. Penny and I had managed to schedule our wedding weekend during the biggest protest gatherings Edinburgh had ever seen. Don't worry—my best man would make sure to bring it up in his toast. The Group of Eight (G8) summit was about to take place near Edinburgh, so the attendees would include the leaders of the richest, most powerful countries in the world.

And so, the next day, there were between 175,000 and 250,000 people marching through the center of the city, protesting against what they saw as the developed world's unfair treatment of the developing world. The "Make Poverty History" campaign was popular in Scotland and throughout the U.K., and grandmothers from church groups were walking alongside college students and families and politicians, blowing whistles and carrying signs.

We all spent the day maneuvering through the marching lines, but it wasn't until the following night, wedding eve, that everyone came together. This was our rehearsal dinner, and the mingling was fun enough that when we had to leave, it didn't seem like we'd been there very long. But sleep was something we all needed, because tomorrow we'd have the protests to contend with.

That's right, the protests. Again.

The wedding was scheduled to take place on the same day that thousands of anti-capitalists, not satisfied with the ordinary protest march from two days before, were contemplating being a tad more confrontational. The vast majority of them weren't Scottish, but were coming in from all over Europe. The police were going to be out in full force, and the newspapers speculated about masked troublemakers roving about. And there was reason to speculate: A few years earlier, at a G8 summit in Genoa, Italy, riots and protests and police had left hundreds of people injured.

I was still asleep in a nearby neighborhood when Penny opened her eyes, took a look out the morning window at Edinburgh Castle, and watched my sister Brittany's face light up when she awoke. The streets were still quiet as the hairdressers and makeup artists did their fabulous work, but that fabulous work took a little longer than expected, and as noon approached it became clear that Penny and her bridesmaids were falling behind The Schedule.

Soon they were standing in front of our hotel in the city center, and a few cabs pulled up, but Penny's best friend Liz had to run upstairs to get something. Penny told the others to go ahead, and they said OK—Penny, Liz and Brittany would be in another cab behind them, and they'd all meet at the reception site, out in the country, where they'd get dressed, and then cars would pick them up and take them to the church.

But just after the cabs pulled away, the reports started coming in. The protesters were coming out earlier than expected, and they were headed in this direction. Penny, Liz and Brittany waited as a line formed behind them, but no cabs were in sight, and even if there had been, no one was sure that they'd be able to get through the barricades that were now up and down the block. Twenty, thirty minutes went by. The Schedule loomed.

Suddenly, police were sprinting toward them from the left, followed by journalists with cameras, and the police were yelling, "If you're not part of this, get out now!" Then Penny looked right and saw protesters turning the corner and heading toward her. The police intercepted them and held them off with their shields, but the protesters kept trying to push their way through, yelling and chanting and whistling. The three main newspapers, on the following day, would carry front-page images with headlines that read:

THE NIGHTMARE COMES TRUE
**LIVE HATE: After the Love-In, the Mob Attacks
Batons Drawn in the Battle of Princes Street**

For the first time, Penny let herself imagine that things just might not work out. Actually, now that she thought about it, there was a pretty good chance that things weren't going to work out. Her face showed it, and Liz looked at her and said, "Everything's going to be fine."

But the loud line of protesters and police was heaving closer and closer to them, and after a few more moments, Penny allowed herself to say it: "We might not get there in time."

"No," Liz said. "No. We will. Because we have to."

Then a man in plainclothes wearing an earpiece walked up and asked if they were all right. The bellhop told him, "Today's this lady's wedding day, and I can't get her out of the city!" The man introduced himself as Paul, and said he was a private security officer, working that day for a company across the street. He said he'd be able to help, and got on his phone. The protesters and police were coming closer.

After a few moments, Paul's coworker Neil ran up and said, "I think we've got a car for them," and a few seconds later, a little hatchback arrived. Their coworker Andrew stepped out of the car. He'd be the driver for the afternoon.

"Sorry, ma'am," Paul said. "This is the best we could find."

"Paul," Penny responded, "I'd take this car if you had to strap me to the top of it."

She thanked the three of them again and again, and offered them money for their trouble, but they wouldn't accept it. "You just need to make it to your wedding," Paul said, and he tapped the top of the car as it started moving down the street.

At each police barricade, Andrew pointed toward Penny and told the policeman, "She's going to be late for her wedding," and each time the policeman smiled and lifted the barricade so they could get by. And soon they were speeding out of the city, passing every car and laughing. They were there within twenty minutes, and Penny insisted that Andrew, Paul and Neil come to the wedding.

The rest of us, though, were back in the city still. Sitting in our rented bus in Charlotte Square, wearing suits and dresses. Bait, in other words.

Everyone was here except for Namjoo, husband of Penny's cousin Armita, who was one of the bridesmaids. Armita had been with the rest of the bridal party, getting made up, and had climbed into one of those cabs just before the protesters showed up. Namjoo was supposed to be here by now, but his phone wasn't working, so I had no way of contacting him.

But if I could have called him, he would have had this to say:

Ryan, Namjoo here. You should just go without me, because I don't know if I'm going to make it. After Armita joined up with Penny and the rest of the bridesmaids, I had an hour or two to spare, so I thought about all the places in the center of Edinburgh where I could go, and I settled on a place where I knew the protesters wouldn't bother me.

Starbucks.

So I'm standing in line, waiting to order my drink, and the next thing I know, there's this commotion behind me. The employees were locking the front door. And a few seconds later, all these protesters were banging on the door. But they didn't try to break in. They stood there like they were besieging us. And they weren't wearing black masks. Strangest thing: They were dressed like clowns, and they were doing cartwheels and handstands.

Anyway, we all stayed inside, hoping they'd move on to some other store, but they stayed. Then the manager told us there was a side exit that the protesters maybe didn't know about, and he took us there. He opened the door slowly, saw no clowns, and let us take off.

I'm already late for the bus in Charlotte Square, so I'm just going to take a train out to Linlithgow. No need to worry about me.

But I, Ryan, sitting in that bus in Charlotte Square, only knew that Namjoo wasn't here yet. We were supposed to leave forty minutes ago. If I gave the bus driver the go-ahead, I'd be The Guy Who Lost Namjoo, but if I waited any longer, I'd be The Guy Who Had to Cancel His Own Wedding.

With the permission of Penny's family, I went for the go-ahead option, and as it turned out, we were able to make it out of the city without any trouble: The protesters had moved on to another neighborhood. Within twenty minutes, we could see the 18th century townhouses of Linlithgow on both sides. Together, we all walked up a cobblestoned hill to the church, with its spire and pocked stones.

The church stood next to the ruins of Linlithgow Palace, and had been built over the course of the 15th and early 16th centuries for the Scottish royal family. Here, in 1513, King James IV was praying when a spirit appeared before him and warned him not to invade England, but he ordered an invasion anyway, and was killed at the Battle of Flodden Field. Here, Mary, Queen of Scots was baptized in 1542, after being born in the palace. Here, Namjoo strolled up with time to spare, fresh from the train station.

And soon, standing in a passageway off to the side of the altar, I could hear the bagpipe as Penny arrived outside. Standing at the altar, I watched them come down the aisle toward me, the ones who felt like home—my mom and stepdad, my brothers and my sister, and then Penny and her mom, who took my hand and placed it into her daughter's.

A few hours later, while we were all finishing up dessert, someone came over to tell Penny we had a few visitors, and in walked Andrew, Paul, and Neil. Penny and I got up and announced who they were, and there was a long round of applause from everyone.

We invited the three of them to stay, but no, they had to go. And as they turned to leave, Paul shook my hand and said, "You'd better take good care of her—she's got family in Scotland now."

CHAPTER 5

LIKE A GHOST

I woke up the next morning in a cottage down the road from where we'd had the reception, with the odd sensation of a ring on my finger. Penny and I stepped outside onto the back porch, overlooking a little loch. Warm sunshine, and I yawned. The only other sound was the quacking of ducks every once in a while, and a breeze. No more protesters, no more wedding planning.

Just two suitcases and the Scottish Highlands.

A train took us out of Edinburgh, west to Glasgow, and then slowly north, along Loch Lomond and up to the small town of Crianlarich, then west again, through Glen Orchy and the Pass of Brander. Now the signs were in English and Gaelic. Houses had lochs for front yards and mountains for back yards. The sky was dark blue, and mists were settling down over the mountains, which sloped down to meet beneath our feet, like they were cradling us as we made our way through them.

It was nearly dark when we pulled into Oban, a port town on the west coast, and saw the gray waves between us and the

Isle of Kerrera, out on the horizon. We found George, a taxi driver who was willing to take us out to our bed and breakfast—an old farmhouse, surrounded by sheep, on the other side of a loch and in the hills.

Over the next few days, our muscles worked out their knots, until they felt massaged, drowsy. Our minds slowed down. Walking up and down the hills, and sitting by the loch, and talking over long breakfasts and dinners, we got to know our new pace. My five o'clock shadow became stubble and then a thin beard.

And all around was the chance, like a ghost, that an ancestor had walked here. This far west, this far north, some MacDonalds must have lived. Maybe right here, beneath the ruins of Dunollie Castle, my ancestors had a home, with this cold, loch water almost at their feet. Maybe right here, in the yard of this medieval priory, one of them was buried in an unmarked grave, or perhaps the stone lost its inscription centuries ago. Perhaps one of them knew this heather mountain, the one Penny and I climbed and sat atop as we watched rain come down across the green hills in the distance. Every corner hid a hint, like someone else just might be lurking.

Soon we drove northwest to the village of Mallaig, where we inched our rental car onto a ferry to the Isle of Skye, one of the old MacDonald strongholds. Mist drizzled around us every once in a while as we stood up on deck. The water we were cutting through was clear and blue-gray and cold, and seagulls followed above us, coasting and veering. We could see the island in the distance, parts of it hidden behind a few wisps of fog, getting closer, light green and dark green and wooded.

Once ashore, we drove down the road to our bed and breakfast, which used to be a hunting lodge for the chiefs of the MacDonalds of Sleat. Now it's the home of Godfrey MacDonald, High Chief of Clan Donald, and his wife Lady Claire. Since I wasn't named MacDonald, I could go in quietly, without anybody thinking of me as some long lost cousin. But if a few ancestral clues fell into my lap, I wouldn't exactly protest. I was almost working undercover.

No kilted chief was at the door—he and Lady Claire were away—but his genealogy was hanging on the wall nearby. Penny and I looked both ways before reading over it, like we were about to shoplift. It was big, framed, written in red and black calligraphy. There was our host at the bottom: Godfrey James MacDonald, 8th Lord MacDonald. Our eyes followed the links upward, from son to father to grandfather. No room was given for women, except as wives. We traced the names back, from the 19th century to the 18th to the 17th: Godfrey William MacDonald, Alexander MacDonald, Donald Breac MacDonald, chiefs of the MacDonalds of Sleat. The 16th century chiefs of Sleat were here, too, and the medieval Lords of the Isles.

Moving further up the chart, we saw the name of Angus Og, the man who fought alongside King Robert the Bruce at the Battle of Bannockburn in 1314. And here was Angus Og's grandfather Donald, the source of the clan's name, and the man from whom all MacDonalds are said to descend. At the top of the chart, sitting alone above the rest, was Donald's grandfather Somerled, who came from the medieval,

Viking-Gaelic culture of the islands of the Hebrides, and who founded the MacDonald dynasty in the 12th century by conquest. Twenty-five generations connected him to our host, Lord Godfrey.

As we ate dinner that night, some of those ancestors seemed to be looking at us. Their portraits, mostly from the 18th and 19th centuries, took up the walls in the dining room. A man with brown hair stood, knowingly, in his military uniform. Ladies and gentlemen wore white, powdered wigs. In a gilded frame were two young boys wearing tartan, sons of the chief, posing with their golf clubs.

Walking around the house and the grounds, it wasn't difficult to imagine those people being here. The chiefs and their guests must have walked through this door, right here, when returning from a hunt. Over there, by that beach, must have been where ships came in. The sitting room was right for coffee and hot tea in the afternoons. The library was right for thumbing through histories of Clan Donald. Even now, in the summer, it was cool enough in the evenings for a fire in the fireplace, and for whiskey before dinner.

But I still hadn't forgotten Grandma's you-don't-fool-me look. I still didn't see how my family was entitled to this red, blue and green tartan. We didn't grow up surrounded by Gaelic names, and our history lessons were about Abraham Lincoln rather than James IV, and our landscapes had always been watered by ponds and lakes rather than lochs and firths. We were spinning a story about ourselves that wasn't necessarily true. Most of us felt what seemed to be a genuine connection to this particular Highland clan, but I wouldn't let myself forget how easy it is to believe something is real, not because it is, but because we want it to be, because we want to be part of the club.

Then again, distant places aren't as distant as they used to be. With globalization, once obscure locales and ways of life have become more and more real, and the exotic has inched closer to the day-to-day. Our nationality seems less like a given and more like just one possibility among others. If any of us can find a new religion, if any of us can move away for good, then why can't we have a bond to the lands of our ancestors?

The problem is that those far off lands don't speak so much to *our* lives as to the lives of our ancestors. My family might wear the MacDonald tartan, but if we were dropped down into the 16th century Highlands, when a tartan signaled a deeply held allegiance, we'd be seen as aliens, with our tans and our body language and our attitudes. Even if your ancestors left more recently, how can you help but be embedded in your own time and place? How can you leap outside of yourself?

These questions were on the mind of Paul Basu, author of *Highland Homecomings*, who talked to people from the U.S., Canada, Australia and elsewhere who'd journeyed to the Scottish Highlands so that they could be in the places where their ancestors had lived. They were trekking to an ancestor's deserted cottage, or to a village where their great-great-grandparents lived before emigrating across the ocean, or to an ancient graveyard of their clan. And again and again, they told Basu that this wasn't an ordinary vacation—it wasn't a stranger's glimpse at a new place. One of them wrote: "I am not, and never will be, a tourist in Scotland."

Don, from Ohio, was visiting his ancestors' lands in Strathnaver. Basu asked him why he'd decided to come here, and Don responded: "Because this is where I'm from. Not physically. I didn't physically come from here, I wasn't physically born here, but *this is where I'm from*, if you can understand that....so that not only am I proud of being a Scot because of my family, but I'm proud of being a Scot because of this. This is where they lived. Because of the battles and that kind of thing that the clan had fought. I'm part of that clan. That's who I am."

And Brenda, from Ontario, was traveling through the isles where her ancestors might have lived. Her husband and daughter had stayed behind, so that she could make the trip on her own. Brenda told Basu, "I just feel so lucky to be here. And this is the real me. At home, I mean of course that's the real me—don't get me wrong—and I love my family and my life and I'm very proud of my life at home. But this is where...I don't want to say this is where my heart is. It goes deeper. My heart is with my child and my husband....My *soul* is here. It's deeper. It's like no one can take that away."

After just two days on the Isle of Skye, a few voices in me were starting to sound like Don and Brenda, and the next morning, Penny and I set off for the Clan Donald Centre, just a short drive down the road to the south. On one of the old estates of the MacDonalds of Sleat, looking out over the bay to the mainland, it has a museum and library devoted to the clan, and the ruins of the castle where some of Lord Godfrey's portraited ancestors once lived.

First up was the restaurant, for an early lunch. Sitting at a window table, we gazed at the clan crests and mottos displayed like banners above us, official seals of past kingdoms: MacDonnell of Antrim, MacDonald of Ardnamurchan, of Clanranald, of Dunivaig, Glencoe, Glengarry, Keppoch, Sleat. While I bit into my sandwich, Penny started speculating. "I wonder which branch your family's from."

I looked up at the crests and Latin mottos and said, "Who knows?" If I deserved a clan crest, it was for the McDonalds of Right Outside Troy, Missouri.

"I know," she said. Silence for a few more moments, except for my munching. "But still. I just have a feeling it might be Keppoch, for some reason."

Now we walked down a path to the museum and followed the MacDonald story: The Viking invasions, the rise of Somerled and the Lords of the Isles, the battles against other clans and against the Scottish and English crowns, the government's massacre of the MacDonalds of Glencoe, the rebellion of 1745, and then the 18th and 19th century dispersals of Highland people all around the globe, known as the Highland Clearances.

There were weapons, poems, jewelry, paintings. I reminded myself that my ancestors might have been part of all of this, but as we looked at the acre of castle ruins, with mountains in the distance, I thought of Grandma and Grandpa's little house back in Chatham, with its flat, mowed lawn surrounded by prairie to the horizon.

At the museum, we'd come across a sign advertising a lecture to be given that afternoon by a man named Bryan Sykes. He was a geneticist at Oxford, and his talk would explore how DNA can shed light on people's ancestry. We walked in and sat down a few minutes before it was supposed to start.

The room was small, fitting about forty fold-up chairs, but most of them were full when Sykes came in with his young son. He was in his 50s, with crinkled eyes, and he was dressed for summer—jeans and a short sleeve shirt. Part of the year, he and his family lived here on Skye, and many of the locals knew him.

He mentioned that his books *The Seven Daughters of Eve* and *Adam's Curse* had mostly been written at his home here, where Sorley MacLean once lived. MacLean was perhaps the greatest Gaelic poet of the 20th century, and he'd passed away several years earlier. When Sykes mentioned his name, there was a murmur behind us—MacLean's wife was sitting in the back, smiling. "Ah, there you are, Renee, sorry I didn't see you," Sykes said. He spoke like a professor during office hours. English, and kind.

He began talking about mitochondrial DNA, which each of us (men and women alike) receives from our mother, and which our mother, in turn, received from *her* mother, who received it from *her* mother, and so on. Our mitochondrial DNA bears the signs of one line of women—our mother to our grandmother to our great-grandmother—stretching hundreds and thousands of years back. Over generations, this DNA undergoes slight mutations, so scientists can estimate how closely related two people are by comparing whether they share particular mutations, passed down by their common ancestor. The more mutations two people share, the more recent their shared ancestry.

The mirror image of mitochondrial DNA, Sykes said, is Y-chromosome DNA. It's passed along from father to son, rather than from mother to child. While both women and men inherit mitochondrial DNA, only men inherit Y-chromosome DNA, since only men have a Y-chromosome in the first place. And for some reason, Y-chromosome DNA mutates much more often than mitochondrial DNA does.

This means that two people's mitochondrial DNA might show the same mutations, but because those mutations happen relatively rarely, there's no way to be sure that they occurred recently on the family tree, or long ago. By contrast, when two men's Y-chromosomes show the same mutations, it suggests a more recent common ancestor, because if their shared ancestor lived many generations ago, we'd expect to find a lot of mutations that these two men *didn't* have in common. Mitochondrial DNA measures two people's shared ancestry in terms of millenia, while Y-chromosome DNA can measure it in terms of centuries, even decades.

And what better laboratory for studying the Y-chromosome's workings, Sykes said, than a Highland clan whose power structure, whose traditions, whose name were all founded on patrilineal descent? A few years earlier, he and his research team had been gathering DNA samples from Scottish volunteers, and they'd noticed a curious pattern: A certain DNA signature, generally rare, seemed to be showing up more frequently in men with the MacDonald surname.

What's more, they noticed, it was showing up in men

named MacDougall and MacAllister. Sykes's research student Jayne Nicholson pointed out that all three clans—not just the MacDonalds—were said to be descended from Somerled, the man who sat at the top of that genealogy Penny and I were reading in Lord Godfrey's library a few days before.

To get more data, Nicholson wrote to MacDonalds and MacDougalls and MacAllisters all over Scotland, asking them to scrape the inside of their cheek with the enclosed brush and return it. Almost one hundred men responded, and this particular DNA signature was shared by 18% of the Mac-Donalds, 30% of the MacDougalls, and 40% of the MacAl-listers. Was this the signature of Somerled?

Here's where traditional genealogies came in. There were four living, legally recognized chiefs of Clan Donald, including our honeymoon host Lord Godfrey, and their status was entirely premised on patrilineal succession. Clan MacDou-gall didn't have a chief, but the MacAllisters did. Sykes had his reservations about contacting the four MacDonalds and the MacAllister—what if one or more of them ended up not matching the others? The best way to deal with that poten-tial predicament, he decided, was to promise all five of them that their results would be kept strictly confidential. So he wrote to each of them, explaining his request and enclosing a cheek-swabbing brush.

All five chiefs agreed, and the results were unequivocal: They all matched. The traditional genealogies had been right all along. For each chief, there had been roughly twenty-five generations, father to son, without a single instance of a "non-paternity event." Their Y-chromosome DNA signature was Somerled's, hidden away in every cell of their bodies. It made perfect sense that MacDonalds were less likely to have Somerled's mark than MacDougalls or MacAllisters were— each MacDonald chief owned more land and thus had more clansmen, so more people would have taken that chief's name despite having a different patrilineal ancestry.

Penny and I were thinking the same thing as we left the room after Sykes' talk. Grandma's younger brother, my great-uncle Chuck, inherited his Y-chromosome DNA signature from his dad, my great-grandpa Lee McDonald. And if there hadn't been any non-paternity events along the way, Chuck's DNA signature would tell us the DNA signature of our McDonald ancestors.

If Chuck would agree to have his DNA tested, we might even be able to find out whether we came from the line of the MacDonald chiefs. We'd know whether Lord Godfrey was my cousin, after all. Maybe Chuck would match one of the chiefs more closely than he matched the others, suggesting that our McDonald ancestors came from a particular branch of the clan. There was a good chance he didn't have the Somerled signature at all, but he could still match others, and that might tell us where our McDonald ancestors came from. I hoped there hadn't been a non-paternity event along the way, but if Chuck's Y-chromosome wasn't a MacDonald Y-chromosome, so be it. I wanted to know whatever the truth turned out to be.

The truth, for now, was that Clan Donald territory wasn't yet a familiar place, no matter how somberly it stunned, no matter how much I wanted to feel at home. You probably already know about this, about being a tourist, when the airport advertisements are only the first of the little estrangements that tell you this place isn't yours. The landscapes and the architecture and the uses of space, all of them, have a different feel. Newspapers mention political controversies you're unaware of, old fights you don't have a stake in. You're removed from the sturdy, steady quiet of belonging.

But that's also why you catch what you ordinarily don't catch. You might notice the chips on old stone turrets, and that cat resting in a window up there, and the phrase you heard from a waiter while you were on your way out. You might begin to sense some things inside you that had been covered up by all the habits and expectations of home.

Maybe those few moments will reach into you more than a thousand days at home could have. Maybe you'll find yourself thinking that this new place is somewhere that would fit you, because there's a comfort that you never saw coming. Home doesn't have a monopoly on belonging—fragments of home are scattered all over, in every place that matters. And that place could be anywhere, and it could even be here, in this far away corner that you'd only imagined, until now.

CHAPTER 6

ANOTHER LOOK

Back in America, back to my habits, I brought out my notes and papers and looked again at my McDonald family tree:

Hiram McDonald (1806-1882), m. Nancy Buchanan
|
William Duncan McDonald (1855-1935), m. Georgianna Wilson
|
Will McDonald (1875-1964), m. Linnie Hagan
|
Lee McDonald (my great-grandpa), m. Mary Bridgewater
|
Betty McDonald (my grandma), m. Don McCord

From Bryan Sykes, I knew that DNA might be able to give me an idea of where my McDonald ancestors came from, but only distant cousins or documents could tell me exactly who those ancestors were. Before the wedding and honeymoon, I'd found Hiram McDonald and his wife Nancy in the Lincoln County, Missouri records beginning in 1836, but I couldn't figure out who Hiram's parents were—my supposed link to Clan Donald.

I went to Ancestry.com again, and searched for any Mc-
Donalds or McDaniels in Lincoln County before 1836. According to the 1830 census, there weren't any households
headed by anyone with those names, but there were two
households headed by people with the name McDanel. I'd
noticed that before, but had figured they weren't related to
Hiram. I'd thought their name was McDanold or something
similar, and besides, neither household was headed by Hiram,
so there was no evidence that these families were connected
to him.

But now I took another look. The Cyrus McDanel household was headed by a young man with a wife and children,
while the Elizabeth McDanel household was headed by a
woman in her forties, and included eleven young adults and
children. Elizabeth was listed one page after Cyrus, so they
probably didn't live too far from each other.

Then I noticed something from the Missouri marriage
records at Ancestry.com. No McDonalds or McDaniels got
married in Lincoln or Pike Counties until 1829, but between
1829 and 1846 there were nine: Betsy, Rebecca, Hiram, Darius, Thomas, James, Patsy, Nancy and Ezekiel. And eight of
the nine got married after 1830. Were these eight people
among the eleven young adults and children in the 1830 Elizabeth McDanel household? Were they all Elizabeth's children,
including my ancestor Hiram?

Maybe. And maybe, by looking at the early Lincoln and
Pike County records, I'd be able to uncover some connections
among all these McDonalds and McDaniels.

I started by focusing on those 1830 census entries for the Elizabeth McDanel and Cyrus McDanel households. Cyrus had been born between 1800 and 1810, and Elizabeth had been born between 1780 and 1790, so she was old enough to be his mother. But Cyrus wasn't listed among the nine McDonalds or McDaniels who'd gotten married in Lincoln or Pike Counties in the 1830s and 1840s. In fact, no one named Cyrus McDonald or McDaniel had gotten married anywhere in Missouri prior to 1830.

Then I looked at the 1820 census and discovered that there'd been no McDonalds or McDaniels living in Lincoln County at the time, which meant that Cyrus could have gotten married outside of Missouri in the 1820s and then moved to Lincoln County by 1830—while still being Elizabeth's son. This didn't prove that he *was* her son, but it showed that he might have been.

Now I looked at the names of the people who were listed next to Elizabeth in the 1830 census. Maybe she lived near them because of some family connection; maybe they'd moved to Lincoln County and bought land together. I wrote down their names and then looked them up in the online Lincoln County records. No luck. No marriages with McDonalds or McDaniels, no land sales or other transactions involving Elizabeth.

But then I did the same thing for Cyrus, who was one page away from Elizabeth in that 1830 census. The list read: Samuel K. Tilford, Ezekiel Downing, Cyrus McDanel. And as soon as I saw the name Tilford, I searched the Missouri marriages again at Ancestry.com. There it was: Liza Ann Tilford and Hiram McDonald, married on February 1, 1833 in Lincoln County.

My ancestor Hiram had married Liza Ann Tilford three years before he'd married my ancestor Nancy Buchanan. I'd seen this before, and had assumed that Liza Ann had died young, without any children.

Now I looked in the 1850 census, which was the first to list every member of a household, and saw that the only Tilford household in Lincoln County was headed by Samuel K., now aged sixty-eight, living with his wife and three adult children. I glanced over the names of the children, and then I came across the youngest person in the household. She was a fifteen-year-old girl named Eliza A. McDonald.

Hiram and Liza Ann had a daughter together. Liza Ann almost certainly died when her daughter Eliza was very young, and then Eliza was raised in the household of the Tilfords, who were probably her grandparents. But why wasn't Eliza brought back into Hiram's family, at least once he married Nancy?

I didn't have an answer yet, but maybe all of this told a story about Hiram's origins. I now knew that Cyrus McDaniel/McDonald, who seemed to be a son of Elizabeth, had lived just one farm away from Hiram's future wife and in-laws. I noticed, too, that there were two men aged twenty to twenty-nine in Cyrus' 1830 household. One was Cyrus, but the other could have been Hiram.

And if Hiram had lived with Cyrus, that could explain how Hiram had come to know Liza Ann. Maybe Cyrus and Hiram had done some work for Samuel K. Tilford and had sat down to lunches with the Tilford family. Maybe Hiram used to walk over to the Tilford house, where he was welcomed, and exchanged glances with Liza Ann while her parents hopefully weren't looking.

No matter how this happened, exactly, it seemed that Hiram had met Liza Ann through Cyrus—here was a McDaniel/McDonald who was Liza Ann's neighbor, who was likely to know the Tilford family. Associating with the same people, living near them and working with them and marrying into their families, was to be expected of two brothers.

I couldn't believe that I'd missed this before.

Then I moved on to Ezekiel Downing, who was living between Cyrus McDaniel/McDonald and Samuel K. Tilford in 1830. Was he linked to Cyrus or Elizabeth or Hiram in any way? My trusted guide, Google, took me back to the Lincoln County GenWeb site, the same place where, before the wedding, I'd found the transcription of Hiram and Nancy's gravestone at the Bryant Creek Cemetery. Now I found a burial place called the Ezekiel Downing Cemetery, with just thirty-two names, a tiny census of the dead. The graveyard must have been on Ezekiel Downing's land, and there were a number of Downings listed, including Ezekiel himself ("b: Aug. 25, 1795; d: Jan. 22, 1849"). But toward the bottom I saw: "Eliza Ann McDONALD – b: Aug. 1, 1834; d: June 22, 1879."

Hiram's daughter from his first marriage had been buried in the same little graveyard as the Downings, who lived next to Cyrus in 1830. This suggested that Hiram and Cyrus both had a connection to Ezekiel Downing—another little piece of evidence that they were brothers.

I clicked back to the Lincoln County GenWeb site and saw that there was one other transcription of the gravestones at the Ezekiel Downing Cemetery. I clicked on a link that took me to the new list, and it mentioned how the cemetery got its name: "Located on the original Ezekiel Downing land which has been in the family since 1816." I began reading the names, and recognized them from earlier. But I came across one name that the first transcriber had missed: "Elizabeth A. McDONALD - b: 1786; d: 1853 w/o John."

Elizabeth McDonald. *Wife of John.* The birth year of 1786 matched the 1830 census record for Elizabeth McDanel, the one I suspected was the mother of Hiram, Cyrus, and the rest—the census record said Elizabeth McDanel had been born between 1780 and 1790. If these two Elizabeths were one and the same, then here was another reason to think she was Hiram's mother; she was buried in the same small cemetery as Hiram's daughter Eliza.

The Lincoln County GenWeb site even described where the Ezekiel Downing Cemetery and the Bryant Creek Cemetery were: Right down the road from each other. Hiram was buried near Elizabeth and his daughter Eliza, and this was one more clue linking Hiram to Elizabeth.

And if Elizabeth *were* Hiram's mother, then John McDonald was almost certainly his father.

So could I find any records proving that the 1830 Elizabeth McDanel was identical to the Elizabeth McDonald buried in the Ezekiel Downing Cemetery? I searched in the 1840 census at Ancestry.com, and found no Elizabeth McDonalds or McDaniels in Lincoln County or Pike County. But in the household of Ezekiel McDaniel, one of the McDonalds/McDaniels who got married in the 1840s, there was a woman in her fifties. This could have been Elizabeth, but it could have been another woman—perhaps Ezekiel's mother-in-law.

So I turned to the 1850 census, which was the first to list every household member. And there, living with Ezekiel, was Elizabeth McDaniel, age sixty-seven. She had to be his mother: She had his surname, and she was forty-two years older than he was. There was no other Elizabeth McDonald or McDaniel living in the area in 1850, so this Elizabeth was almost certainly the same one who was buried in 1853 in the Ezekiel Downing Cemetery.

And then I saw how the 1840 census showed Cyrus living next to James, another McDonald/McDonald who got married in the 1830s. And in 1850, Hiram was living close to the father and brother of Darius McDonald's wife. And then Google took me to a site that mentioned the founding of the Smyrna Presbyterian Church in Pike County. Among the first seven members of the church were Cyrus McDonald, Darius McDonald and Elizabeth McDonald.

Penny had been working late that night, but I'd been able to duck out early. When she came home, I got up from the computer and hugged her, and said I was sorry she had to work late, and she said it was no big deal, she was just tired.

She was putting away her coat and shoes, and I asked, "You've had dinner already, right?"

"Right."

Silence. Husband stepping away, back toward the computer.

"So," she asked, "is there something you want to tell me?"

Furrowed brow. "Well, I think I might have figured out who Hiram McDonald's parents were." And it came out like a two-minute presentation:

- An Elizabeth McDaniel or McDonald was in Lincoln County, Missouri in the 1830 census, along with several young adults and children. Then, in the 1830s and 1840s, several McDaniels/McDonalds got married in the area, including Hiram.

- This same Elizabeth lived with Ezekiel McDaniel in 1850, so she just had to be his mother. Ezekiel was one of those young, married McDaniels/McDonalds, so the fact that Elizabeth was his mother suggests that she was the mother of at least some of the others.

- This Elizabeth from the 1830 and 1850 censuses was almost certainly the Elizabeth McDonald who died in Lincoln County in 1853, and whose husband was John McDonald.

- The other McDaniel/McDonald in the 1830 Lincoln County census was Cyrus, a young man who was living very close to Liza Ann Tilford, whom Hiram married just a few years later.

- In that 1830 census, Cyrus was living next to Ezekiel Downing, and Elizabeth McDonald, wife of John, is buried on Ezekiel's land. So is Eliza Ann McDonald,

Hiram's daughter from his first marriage.

- Like Hiram, James McDonald and Darius McDonald got married in the 1830s and 1840s, and Cyrus lived next to James, while Hiram lived close to Darius' in-laws. And Cyrus, Darius and Elizabeth started a church together.

These connections couldn't just be coincidences. It seemed like Hiram *had* to be the son of Elizabeth and John. Cyrus, Darius, Ezekiel and the rest of them *had* to be Hiram's siblings. All the facts fit into that story.

Still, what if there were some facts out there that didn't fit into the story? I hadn't found any, but that didn't necessarily mean they didn't exist. Hiram might have been related to John and Elizabeth in some way, but wasn't their son. Hiram could have been their nephew, for instance, migrating to Lincoln County because his parents had passed away.

To know for sure that Hiram was the son of John and Elizabeth, I needed some piece of clear evidence, something to unwind the doubts—Elizabeth's will, for instance, or the court records concerning her estate. But none of these were online. Maybe there wasn't an answer to the question of Hiram's ancestry, but if there were one, it would only be found in one place: Lincoln County, Missouri.

Time for a road trip.

CHAPTER 7

HIGHLANDERS

The Lincoln County GenWeb site said that all public records were at the courthouse in the county seat of Troy, so I'd probably be able to walk in and search, for a few hours, for a day, for as long as it took. And the cemetery transcriptions described where Elizabeth, Eliza, Hiram, and Nancy were buried, so I knew which roads to go down, and where to pull off and look around for telltale trees and houses and hopefully find the four of them. Their gravestones might even reveal something that the online transcriptions had missed.

In a couple of months, I'd be going home to Chatham, in central Illinois. Driving southwest on I-55 and across the Mississippi River to St. Louis would be easy, just a 90 minute drive, and it wouldn't be hard to get from there to Lincoln County. I found a hotel in Troy, close to the courthouse and a short drive out into the country, where the cemeteries were.

As I planned the trip, though, DNA was on my mind. I could end up searching across Lincoln County for days and still find nothing, because no one had thought to write down who Hiram's parents were. Or maybe someone had written it down decades ago, but the pages were now in some unknowing stranger's attic, or maybe the pages had been thrown away or burned.

A few cells from the inside of one man's cheek, on the other hand, might reveal nearly everything: Generation after generation had passed along that DNA signature to Chuck, Great-grandpa Lee's son, Grandma's brother. There was no way to forget it, or hide it, or change it. There was no arguing with DNA. A report from a DNA company might reveal that my ancestors came from Clan Donald, and that they had the signature of the clan chiefs, and that they came from one particular place in the Highlands of Scotland.

Or not.

Because what if all of that turned out to be a fantasy? Bryan Sykes had said that about 20% of men with the Mc-Donald/MacDonald surname had the DNA signature of Somerled, the 12th century Highland king from whom the Clan Donald chiefs are descended. But this meant about 80% of McDonald/MacDonald men *didn't* have Somerled's signature.

And on the Isle of Skye, leaving Sykes' lecture, I'd recognized it. Chuck probably wouldn't have the Somerled signature, but that didn't matter, I'd said: I just wanted to know the truth.

Well, now I wasn't so sure.

You can imagine the scenario. Chuck's DNA matches the DNA of a man—let's call him John Miller—whose great-great-grandparents Thomas and Elizabeth Miller were good old friends of my ancestors Hiram and Nancy McDonald in Lincoln County, Missouri.

Clearly, there'd been a "non-paternity event" here, but there's still hope for that MacDonald tartan, there's still hope for my ancestor Nancy's honor, because maybe Hiram had been the one who'd strayed. Yes, maybe that alleged descendant of Thomas Miller matched Chuck only because he had *Hiram's* DNA signature, a McDonald one.

But then I go down the list of DNA matches, and all the men have the name Miller, and none have the name McDonald, and here's introducing you to your new ancestor Thomas Miller.

I could already hear myself making the call: "Hello, is this David, the wedding photographer? Hi, I was wondering. Do you remember that tartan, the one that pretty much everybody in my family was wearing? Yeah, do you think you could airbrush it out of all the pictures?"

Besides, even if Chuck's DNA didn't bring a non-paternity revelation, there was a chance that he wouldn't match anyone at all. And even if the cheek swab did yield some cousins, those cousins might be really distant. Chuck might match a man on some DNA markers, but *not* match him on quite a few, which would mean that this man was related to us, but had an ancestral line that had branched off from ours a long time ago—perhaps five hundred years in the past. A match like that wouldn't be close enough to reveal who my 17th and 18th century ancestors were, and where they lived before coming to America.

So when I searched for a DNA company, I was already prepared: Don't be surprised if Chuck doesn't have the Somerled signature, don't be shocked if your ancestors have the name Miller or Johnson or Weiskopf, and most of all, don't be surprised if the DNA dissolves into an Anglo-Scottish-Irish fog.

Googling the words "MacDonald" and "DNA" brought me to a website for people who had reason to believe that their ancestors came from Clan Donald. The project had over three hundred members, all of whom had submitted their DNA. There was even a press release from the project coordinator, Mark MacDonald, spelling out Somerled's DNA signature. All I needed to do was persuade Chuck to participate.

Even though Chuck was my great-uncle, he was only three years older than Mom, so he'd always been more of an uncle to me, and I called him Uncle Chuck. He was a military guy, and he had stories about bar fights in various parts of the world, but now he was retired from all that. Officially, at least.

I often spent time with him when I went back to Chatham, but I didn't have his phone number or email address, so I gave Mom a call. She was the first woman to be elected mayor of Chatham, and she ran a tight ship. She knew how to persuade. "I think Chuck probably wouldn't mind," she said. "I'll talk to him."

And soon, Uncle Chuck was sitting at Mom's house, opening his mouth and saying "aaah" while she swabbed the inside of his cheek with the little plastic scraper. "Well," Mom told me after the operation was over, "we'll just send back this scraper and see what happens."

Several weeks went by, and one day I woke up and had a glass of water, and poured the grinds into the coffee maker, and while the coffee brewed, I looked at my email. There was a message from the DNA company. Uncle Chuck's results were in.

I clicked on the link in the email, and it took me to a website that had been set up for us. Here was the DNA signature of my McDonald ancestors, a number for each gene. Here was the DNA signature of my great-grandpa Lee, and of his father Will, and of *his* father William Duncan, and of *his* father Hiram. I went back to the website that listed the Somerled signature, and wrote it down in my notebook, number by number.

Then I started with the first of Uncle Chuck's genes, checking it against its Somerled counterpart. The first few matched, but then there was a mismatch, and then a few more matches, but then another mismatch. As I moved from one gene marker to the next, Chuck's genes showed more and more mismatches against Somerled's, like a baseball team falling further behind with each inning. When I got to the end, there was no doubt. Chuck's DNA signature wasn't even close to the signature of the Clan Donald chiefs.

I was disappointed, and then I felt guilty for being disappointed.

Not knowing how to find out what the results meant, I once again turned to the most time-tested method: I typed Uncle Chuck's DNA signature, every single number, into Google. And I found a post on an Internet message board by Mark MacDonald, the coordinator for the Clan Donald DNA Project, who had access to the DNA signatures of every project participant. In the post, Mark was asking others where a certain DNA signature might have originated: Did it come from Norse Vikings, like Somerled's signature, or was it indigenous to the Scottish Highlands? The signature was almost identical to Chuck's, so it must have come from a cousin of ours. Mark was asking about my family.

The consensus from the other researchers seemed to be that the signature was too rare to tell for sure. Mark thanked them, and as he thanked them, he referred to us as a "small but historically prominent family of MacDonalds."

Small but historically prominent. What did that mean?

I already knew that we weren't descended from the clan chiefs, but maybe "small but historically prominent" meant that we were related to some other famous MacDonald. John MacDonald, the first Prime Minister of Canada? Flora MacDonald, the one who saved Bonnie Prince Charlie by transporting him over the sea? The two brothers in California who started McDonald's?

Mark seemed to be the right person to ask, so I decided to email him. I introduced myself as Chuck's great-nephew, gave him Chuck's DNA signature, and mentioned that my family hadn't yet discovered who our McDonald ancestors were.

When Mark emailed me back, he seemed to make a vague reference to my family's possible origins, but it wasn't quite clear what he was getting at. One thing was clear, though: He wanted to know a little more from me. "What family traditions do you have?" he asked.

I wrote back: As far as I knew, my family hadn't passed down anything about where our McDonald ancestors came from. But I was hoping he might be able to say more about what the DNA results meant. Over the next few hours, I went for a walk, checked my email. Watched the news, checked my email. Thought about dinner, checked my email.

Then Mark's message showed up, and I began reading. I could feel the wet starting in my eyes, building with each sentence, until a tear fell out as I reached the end. Out of about 350 men in the Clan Donald DNA Project, there were only three who matched Uncle Chuck. All three had the name MacDonald, and all three could definitely trace their MacDonald ancestry to one little group of people, who lived for centuries in one particular place.

Glencoe.

I felt like I'd just heard my name for the first time.

CHAPTER 8

PORT NAM MARBH

Bu mhath leam innse dhuibh mu mo mhuinntir, mu 'r dachaigh agus mar a thachair e.

I would like to tell you about my people, about our home, about how it happened.

I have lived in the glen my whole life, but what I know has not come from my eyes alone. It also has come from my father, and from all the bards before him, who remembered the old stories and brought them into a voice. It has come from my mother, who showed me how to watch for every moment in the glen.

But I will not tell you in that soon forgotten tongue, the tongue of my mother and father, and of all my ancestors. No, I will say this in *your* language. In the words of the south, in the language of the English, whose ways are all around me now: Their laws, their forts and signs, their roads made for the marching of redcoats. Their monarch, and their imagining of our history, because they were afraid. Their always spreading habits, their Cromwell and Magna Carta, their scripted dances and walled-away estates, their swarming navy. Their tidy shires.

I still cannot see how this happened, I still cannot believe that they came all the way here and did it. Because our glen, which you would call a valley, is so far north and so far west that it is days away from your Glasgow and your Edinburgh, let alone your London. It is so far north and so far west that when it meets the sea, it meets ocean water that has always remained north of the northern coast of Ireland. It is so far north and so far west that many generations passed before English or Latin or any other language was heard.

Before the English came, before we MacDonalds came, before even the Romans made their noises to the south, the *Feinn* lived here. The *Feinn* were a race of giant men, led by Fionn MacCumhail, father of our great bard Oisín. No one, no man anywhere, could hunt deer as well as the *Feinn*, and this was because of their hounds, who very nearly flew across streams, and went with them up into the mountains. These deerhounds gave our home its name: Glen of the Dogs, *Gleann Comhann*, Glen Coe.

From the south, from *your* south, you will first have to come over the moor of Rannoch. This is flat land for miles. The mountains are far away on the horizon, at first, and the journey will take at least a day. You will find sky all over. The flowers and mosses grow short, and where a tree grows at all, it stands alone, and crooked. You will see no one here, except for a few of the broken men, who belong to no clan. You will hear few sounds, because there are no hills to bring back echoes.

Hundreds of ponds are all about you, and if you were to

see them from atop the highest mountain, they might look like a man's nose, or a cloven log, or three points of an antler. You will walk around pools, sometimes just the size of a bed, and they are your only mirror, as blue or white or grey as the sky is at that moment. Large stones and boulders are upon the ground every so often, as if they had been strewn about in a quarrel among giants.

For more than two hours, you have seen the mountain called *Buachaille Etive Mòr*, coming closer each time you paused, becoming bigger. Soon it is above you, on the left, and it is almost symmetrical, a cragged head of an arrow pointing to the sky. Across from it, to your right, is *Beinn a' Chrùlaiste*, which slopes up from the moor and then steepens as it rises, becoming a wall of rock. Below these two peaks, down in the gap between them, is the way into our glen.

Now the mountains cover a little more of the sun. There is a fog about the peaks, probably, and the mist is settling down, beading up on your skin, making drops upon your clothes. There are the streams in your ears, plopping and flowing. Your shoes will slip upon the heather and ferns.

At first, the way is winding, under the mountains we call *Beinn Bheag* and *Buachaille Etive Beag*. But after a time, the view opens up in front of you, almost as straight as a hallway in a great house, with a high ridge along the right and the Three Sisters looming one after another on the left. The first of the Sisters is *Beinn Fhada*, then *Gearr Aonach,* and then *Aonach Dubh*, which leans over as though it were about to fall upon you.

Rainwater and mistwater are trickling down from the

mountains into streams such as *Allt an t-Seanmhuir* and *Allt Coire Meannarclach*. One of these streams, *Allt Lairig Eilde*, comes down into a waterfall to your left. This becomes the River Coe, and while you walk alongside it, the river takes in more of the brooks from above, and yet more. As you pass through the long hallway, beneath the peaks, you will see that the water quickens across the meadow known as Achtriachtan.

Here, however, the way winds again, with *Sgorr nam Fiannaidh* up above you on the right, and green *Meall Mor* up on the left. Down where you are, a field stretches for a few hundred yards and the river beside you tumbles over rocks. Then, under the cone peak of *Sgorr na Cìche*, with the hills of Ardgour on the horizon, you come to our loch, which becomes the western sea. The ocean, as you call it.

Light comes and goes all over the glen, because almost every time a cloud passes under the sun, the shadow below moves across the mountains. Soon the flowers and grass are in unbroken sun, until another cloud arrives and a new, long shadow rolls across. Even when the sky is wholly blue, some mists come down to cover the mountaintops, and even when the sky is quite full of the grey, a few mountaintops stay clear. For most of the year, the rain is off and on, as well, all day; it will drizzle for a bit, then clear, then come again and build without yet becoming a downpour, and then break for a time until the next, present drizzling.

In spring and summer, the meadows sit, bright green, and the heather stretches with its pink and purple. The streams swell, now, with new water. But the rocks are up there, as well, mute, as they were last year and the year before, and always. In autumn there is the velvet and the auburn, but along the river and even near the brooks, the bright green has not passed. Only in winter do things become almost uniform, when the snow covers the passes below and the peaks above, and the streams ice up and the trees frost over.

No matter the season, no matter how cold, there is one place to which we return. North, out over the waters of the loch, is *Eilean Munde*, the Isle of St. Munda, with ocean waves hitting every shore. This isle is where I will be buried. This is where all of my ancestors lie, and all those who have belonged to the clan of *Iain Abrach*.

But we are not the only ones who bury here. It is not ours alone. To the north of the loch are the Camerons of Callart, and to the southwest are the Stewarts of Ballachulish. The isle has three places where a boat may come ashore, and so there is one rocky beach for each of the three clans: One for the Camerons, one for the Stewarts, one for the MacDonalds. These are called The Ports of the Dead.

I have seen it, when our people gather upon the southern shore of the loch. Her body is carried from her house and brought down into the boat. One man climbs into the boat, and he readies his two oars. The water is cold, always. Our bagpiper begins to play the lament.

There is fog on the water as the piper plays. The isle can hardly be seen. The boat pushes off, and a few more boats follow behind, holding her family and the buriers. There is a hush, and sobs and quiet voices, and the sound of the rowing, with the water passing over the oars, and all around is the piper's lament. But now the pipes are fading as the isle comes closer. Through the fog, the oarsmen are the first to see the port of the MacDonalds, and know they have found the place.

Chapter 9

Just Off the State Highway

Not long after receiving Mark MacDonald's email about the DNA results, I was packing for the trip to Lincoln County, Missouri. There, hopefully, I'd uncover my great-great-great-great-grandpa Hiram McDonald's parents. I'd be a step closer to discovering how my McDonald ancestors came to America, and why, and exactly who they were. The path to Glencoe somehow went through Lincoln County.

I went home to central Illinois, and after a few days, got in the car. Driving southwest toward St. Louis, I saw exit signs for towns I knew: Farmersville, Litchfield, Staunton, Collinsville. Every ten minutes or so, you could look off to the side and see the water tower of a small town, and in between towns were the country roads that run alongside cornfields and soybean fields.

Country roads in Illinois don't wind their way—they form a grid, organized, marking off parcels of land with precision. I could look out over the fields and see a grove of trees a mile away, or a grain silo or a radio tower. There aren't many undiscovered corners here. When it's flat in every direction, all the way to the horizon, the sky looms down at you, so that you're within it, not under it.

I passed under the signs on I-55 that tell you how to get to the suburbs on the Illinois side of the Mississippi River, and soon I was driving over the river, surprised, as I always am, at how big it is. From there, it was a short drive northwest on Highway 61, and then I was nearing Troy, the Lincoln County seat.

I'd never been to Lincoln County, and it seemed that everyone in my family had left by the early 1900s. What I knew about the place came from Internet research. For me, Lincoln County was all about online summaries of marriage records from the 1830s and 1840s, a few historical accounts of the area, my own imaginings of Hiram and Nancy's life together.

And since I'd never experienced the places where my ancestors lived, those places were unmoored from the here and now. My Lincoln County wasn't the county in eastern Missouri with a current population of 47,727, but the setting of a 19th century family tale. Maybe that's why, as I drove into Troy, everything modern felt alien—the billboards advertising new subdivisions, the Jim Trenary Chevrolet dealership.

Eating lunch at Mustang Sally's, I went over the plan for the day. The online transcription of Hiram's gravestone showed that he died in October of 1882, and I'd learned that Lincoln County only recorded deaths in 1883 and 1884, so there wouldn't be a death certificate revealing his parents. But the county courthouse might have a will or a probate record, or maybe a marriage record, showing that Hiram was Elizabeth's son.

After going through the records at the county courthouse, I'd head north out of Troy. Just off the state highway, a few miles out of town, was the Bryant Creek Cemetery, where Hiram and Nancy were buried. Elizabeth was buried just down the road, at the Ezekiel Downing Cemetery. The courthouse would probably close around 5:30, so I'd have enough time to see their graves after that.

I finished my grilled ham and cheese sandwich and drove a few blocks to the county courthouse on Main Street, with its columns and red bricks. I was led past the front desk of the Recorder of Deeds office and down a narrow hallway, and then up a staircase that creaked a little as I walked. The room above felt like an attic—short ceiling, old carpet, muffled voices coming from the office downstairs. For a second or two, the sense came over me that I was in somebody else's house without their permission. I was the only one here.

I'd told myself to look through the wills and probate records first, but I couldn't resist opening one of these old books that contained the wedding records. All these couples, all these names, rendered by 19th century justices of the peace in their cursive handwriting, ink stains here and there.

I ran my hands over the paper every once in a while as I turned the pages, making my way back, from the 1850s to the 1840s. I took out the oldest book, the one that recorded the earliest weddings in the county, and made my way through 1838, to 1837, to an entry that read: "Be it remembered that on the 7th day of April A.D. 1836 was joined in the holy state of matrimony by the undersigned justice Hiram McDonald and Nancy Buchanan. Signed, Brice W. Hammack."

I'd never seen a picture of Hiram or Nancy, and I knew almost nothing about them except their names and some dates, so I was hoping at least to see their signatures, a few marks of individuality that the two of them might have left behind. But only the justice of the peace had signed. And none of the witnesses to the wedding were listed.

If I were going to discover who Hiram's parents were, it would have to be through wills and probate records.

I pulled out the book that included an index of all Lincoln County probate records, organized by the surname of the deceased. I opened it up and found my way to the M's. Maybe, any moment now, I'd see that familiar name, and then in less than a minute I'd be reading a court record listing Hiram as Elizabeth's son.

But I went through all the M's, and there was no Elizabeth McDonald. For some reason, her estate had never gone through probate.

That meant it was on to the wills, in this file cabinet here. These were the originals, organized by date, folded into yellowed envelopes. According to the online transcription of her gravestone, Elizabeth had died in 1853, so I started with the earliest wills, thumbing my way toward the present, and when I came to 1853 without finding any McDonald wills, I felt the first tinges of disappointment. As I went further, it became clear that Elizabeth hadn't left a will.

It almost seemed like she and Hiram never wanted me to know, like they'd tried to make it impossible for me to discover them. Like they'd covered their tracks.

One thing caught my eye, though—Samuel K. Tilford's

will, filed in 1860. Samuel was the one who appeared to be the father of Liza Ann Tilford, Hiram's first wife, and grandfather of their daughter Eliza. I opened up the envelope even though I wasn't his descendant, and had no way of knowing whether he would have minded the intrusion. I scanned over his handwriting, and there it was, a bequest to "my granddaughter Eliza Ann McDonald." Just as I'd expected, Samuel was Liza Ann's father, Hiram's first father-in-law.

Right then, someone called from downstairs: "Just to let you know, we'll be closing in a few minutes."

"Thanks, I'm almost done," I said.

There was still enough time to look for Hiram and Liza Ann's marriage record, so I went back to the old, leather bound books. The entry was dated February 1, 1833, and said that they'd been married "in the presence of James McDonald, Fielding Lewis and James Stone & others." Again, there were no signatures, but James McDonald was probably the same James I suspected of being Hiram's brother.

Still, it was disappointing not to see Elizabeth listed as one of the witnesses. Maybe she was one of the "others." Maybe she wasn't even there—I began to wonder whether she was Hiram's mother after all. If she had been his mother, wouldn't there be *some* record that showed it, somewhere up in this attic?

Quickly, and expecting the nice lady downstairs to come up any second now and be a little less nice, I picked up the book that included the indexes to land records. Maybe Elizabeth and Hiram had bought or sold land together, or to one another, which would give at least a little support to the idea that they'd been mother and son. But even though there were several land sales between Elizabeth and Ezekiel McDonald, and a few between her and Darius McDonald, there weren't any between her and Hiram.

I wanted to stay and read more, hoping some revelation would save the day, but it was time to go. Stepping out of the courthouse, I could feel how the air had cooled in the last few hours, and I could see gray clouds coming in. It felt like I was in a movie whose messages were obvious: Notice how nature mirrors the inner turmoil of the protagonist. Because I knew tracing back Hiram's ancestry was probably a lost cause at this point. Records just hadn't been kept, and I shouldn't have let myself hope that they had been. The link between Hiram and the MacDonalds of Glencoe would have to remain a mystery.

I sat in the car for a minute while looking over my maps. The Ezekiel Downing Cemetery, where Elizabeth was buried, was just a short drive away, but it was on privately owned property, and what if I weren't welcome, or what if the owner weren't home? The Bryant Creek Cemetery, where Hiram and Nancy were buried, was about two miles farther down the road. And from what I could tell, it was open to the public, so I'd go there first.

Map in the right hand, steering wheel in the left, I made my way out of town and then spent a minute or two in that stretch where it's no longer town but not yet country, where billboards and subdivisions run into fields. Soon, though, it was all fields and trees on either side. After a few miles, I turned onto the state highway—a two-lane country road, really, with houses and farmers' fields and lawns right up against it. If you lived here, and you slowed down the car to turn onto your driveway, there'd probably be no one behind you to mind.

I drove slowly, looking around and glancing at the map to get a sense of where I was. Ahead was supposed to be a house, according to an Internet source, and the Ezekiel Downing Cemetery was in a grove of red cedars behind that house, about 200 yards off of the road. I saw the house, and so I slowed even more, trying to get a glimpse of the cemetery, but it was blocked from view by trees and a barn.

Now the road curved, straightened, and after a minute or two, made a bend. The Bryant Creek Cemetery was supposed to be in a grove of trees right by the road, but after a few moments I started to think I'd missed it. I saw a gravel driveway and pulled off to take another look at my map. Just past the cemetery, there was supposed to be a winding path or mini-road. Maybe this driveway was it.

If so, the cemetery would be about a hundred feet back, somewhere in those trees. I couldn't see any signs or gravestones from here, though. It was misting, and quiet, and the gray in the sky brought out a bit of the blue in the grass. I got out and started toward where the cemetery might be. Somebody in a car drove by, probably wondering what I was doing trudging along in wet, six inch grass.

Off of the road was an old fence, barbed all the way along the top. I walked along it for a few moments until I saw what looked like a tombstone.

There it was, the cemetery, nearly concealed in the trees, enclosed by its own fence.

But I needed to find a way through this barbed wire fence on the outside. I came across a gate, but it was chained shut with a lock. And that cow over there was kind of glaring at me. Whoever owned this land apparently didn't want anyone to enter without permission, and I had no way of knowing who the owner was, let alone know how to contact him or her.

Fingering the barbs, I stood for a while, trying to read the inscriptions on stones sitting less than ten yards away. Hiram and Nancy were right *there*, but I was shut out from seeing them. Logic said I shouldn't be surprised, but logic wasn't able to hold back the feeling in me that I was being told I didn't belong here, that I wasn't on the guest list.

Walking toward the car, I thought of just going back into Troy and finding a place to have dinner, recognize reality, call it a day. Still, on my way out, I'd check one more time for the Ezekiel Downing Cemetery down the road, where Elizabeth McDonald was buried—perhaps the mother of Hiram, or perhaps not. Nearing the house again, this time from the opposite direction, I slowed the car down to a crawl, and from this angle I could see the cemetery clearly. It was in a circle of trees, enclosed by a fence, out in the middle of a soybean field behind the house, like an island.

I turned into the driveway, parked and looked around: White house, neatly trimmed lawn, a barn that had an official-looking "1816" printed on it. Hopefully, someone was home, and hopefully, that someone wouldn't think I was crazy.

Here goes.

CHAPTER 10

DÙTHCHAS

Tha fhios agam nach eil cuimhne oirnn aig mòran nach eil a'
fuireach 'nar beanntan 's ri taobh ar n-aibhnichean.

I know that few of you, beyond our streams and mountains, remember us.

Few of you know how our Gaelic would pause when wolves' eyes appeared, or how the River Coe glistened as it pushed along, slowly, like shards of glass. Few know the smell of damp plaid with peat smoke. Few of you know how our men looked as we stood behind our chief on the field, while our axes waited and the bagpipes sang the songs of our fathers, until the signal came and our screams landed upon our enemy and we charged.

If you are to know anything of us, you will first want to know of *these* things, of our ways, our mornings, because these are what they have always wanted to take away from us.

We have rarely numbered more than five hundred or so, and like our ancestors, most of us live in just a few villages tucked beneath the mountains. There is Achtriachtan under the steep face of *Aonach Eagach* on one side, and on the other, the looming of the Three Sisters, near the meeting of the waters, with heather all about. Farther down the glen is the village of Achnacon, where the river twists before the Field of the Dogs. Inverrigan, then, lies quietly away from the river, hidden at the beginning of a little forest, along the stream of *Allt Fhiodan*. Where the glen ends, on the shore of Loch Leven, there are the villages of Invercoe and Carnoch. Both of them, and all of their roofs, can be seen from the burial isle.

Some of the old ways have turned shape, but are still in our memory. They are still here with us. For one, our people never congregated our houses around a manor, or placed them, full of hope, near a market, or scattered them away to fields of wheat. No, our few villages stayed within a full pail's walk from the river, and our houses were made for shelter, not secluded resting, because there are places in the mountains for that, and even places by the loch, where one can sit and see without hearing another person's voice for hours.

We built those houses of stone, with no need of mortar, for the walls were so thick that snow and rain could never enter. Neither could they come through the roof, whose curved timbers carried the water down and away from the earth and thatch above. The fire burned all day, escaping through a hole in the roof, and was smothered with ashes each night, as the embers smouldered beneath. The beds were the earthen floor, or bunches of heather with the brush turned upward and the roots turned down against the ground.

Keeping us warm were the same clothes that covered us during the day. Each one, man and woman alike, had a long, linen shirt called the *léine croich*, which stayed the colour of saffron, even after all the river washings, and it lay under our draping plaid.

Salmon and herring came to Loch Leven, especially in spring and summer, when they flipped about in our nets and came back for cleaning, and then hung above fires. Red deer lived all across the moor of Rannoch and up in the mountains. With luck, one of them fell to a good aim, a good stalk, while sheep and goats remained closer, chomping near our beds and giving clothes and milk. Away from their bleats and teeth, but close enough to our houses, the oats grew in long rows by barley and kale.

For all that, we mostly depended upon our cattle, the long-haired and stocky ones, the ones who could feed so many. The seasons moved around them. All winter, they stayed close to us, near Carnoch, and on the field by Achnacon in the middle of the glen, and on the meadow beside the loch of Achtriachtan. Here we could give them what extra food we had, but we had little to spare. Sometimes, we, too, did not have enough, and it was then that we had to bleed them, to make the black sausages which we first gave to the children, and next to the old. Even when we had enough for ourselves, many of the cattle died in the barren of the cold.

In spring, however, with the grasses growing, they gained their strength and began to fatten as April became May, as we celebrated the festival of *Bealltainn*. Soon after the festival, we herded them eastward, some to the grasses below *Buachaille Etive Beag* and some onto *Am Monadh Dubh*, the Black Mount, the plateau overlooking the moor of Rannoch. There they would graze for months.

Everyone came along with them, adults and children, sleeping in temporary huts called shielings, as the cattle fattened more and the streams filled and dropped into the river below. The men hunted deer and boar, practised as archers, and looked after the cattle, because raiders could creep at any time. The women helped repair the huts at first, and then made butter and cheese and spun wool, and when autumn approached, we all returned with the cattle into the glen.

By sunset of the last day of October, when we celebrated the festival of *Samhuinn*, most of the remaining cattle were killed and salted, and so they would help to bring us through the winter. We celebrated this *Samhuinn*, this harvest, as it always had been celebrated, as it had been celebrated even before the cross came.

Yes, in the early 7th century, Fintan Mundus came to the glen from our cousins in Ireland and brought the Christian faith to us, and we have held fast to Christ. We are, still, unmatched in our devotion.

But we have not let go of the old knowledge. We have not forgotten that our ancestors understood much. They knew that if *An Duine Mor*, a giant man, was seen walking at night, disaster would soon come. A water-bull, stronger and fiercer than any land bound one, lived within the loch of Achtriachtan, and fairies were in the woods. Rowan trees protected against witches. When a person was laid to rest in the burial isle, he had to stand watch over the graves until the next soul was buried there, and at night, from across the loch, people saw lights moving upon the isle. In the River Coe, foretelling sadness, the *Bean Nighe* would show herself, a phantom woman who washed her shrouds in the passing water. We also knew that a few people possessed the *Darna Shealladh*, the Second Sight, which gave them visions that told of the future.

For those who did not have the Second Sight, the plain view could be enough. The plain view told all of our old stories.

It was there, upon the burial isle, that Fintan Mundus once preached, lived, and built his church. Next to it lay *Eilean a' Chòmhraidh*, the Isle of Discussion, where disputes had always been settled. On the field of Achnacon, Fionn Mac-Cumhail and his giant warriors once defeated Viking invaders who had sailed into Loch Leven. When another band of Vikings sailed in, their ship sank at the entrance to that same loch, and although most of the men drowned, their leader survived by clinging to a boulder known as *Clach Pharuig*, which remains visible at low tide. Standing beneath *Aonach Dubh*, the leaning mountain, we could look up and see the cave where Fionn MacCumhail's son Oisín composed his verses.

When we speak of this glen, even now, we use a word that you do not quite have. When I say *dùthchas*, I hear something that your tongue divides into two. You say "home" and "heritage" as though they are two different things.

But for us, *dùthchas* has always been both: My home is my heritage, and my heritage is my home. I am tied to this land because my parents and grandparents were here, and the ancestors as well, in this same glen, walking beside that same loch, walking up into those same hills. Too, I inherited their poems, their principles and allegiances, just as I inherited their land. I brought their convictions into myself just as I came to know the shapes of our peaks, and I have lived in their warnings just as I have lived in their house.

So it is that we have always taken in strangers. Home is so abundant that we can share it with a newcomer, yet never run out. My home, this glen, belongs to me, but it is not a fortress, with a moat of darting eyes or wary questions.

No, it is a place for meeting, for opening, because I have nothing to fear in my own house. I have nothing to hide. I have only welcomes to give, and good herring and venison, and a roof that will keep out every drop of the rain. I have only a good piper, I have only the clear water of the Coe. I have only the shields and swords of the greatest clan, the sons of Conn, who have won battle after battle, and still bow to no one. To close the door to a stranger is to show fear; to let him in is to share my strength.

When we remember the *Feinn*, the giant warriors who once lived here, we speak of courage in battle and prowess in hunting, but also of generosity to newcomers, of feasts that fed any who came, hungry, into the glen. How could Fionn MacCumhail, or any great man, turn away a stranger in need? Imagine being a traveller coming into a far away place for the first time. Imagine being cut off from home, from all of its assurances, its protections. Imagine being away from all of your family, not knowing for certain whether they are alive or dead, not knowing for certain whether all of your children have kept their strength. Imagine not knowing whether you would have enough food.

That is why all Highland people, all of the Gaels, remember Alasdair Ruadh MacGregor, the Chief of the MacGregors. One day, while Alasdair was at home in Glen Strae, his son went hunting with several other MacGregors. Soon they encountered the young chief of Clan Lamont, who happened to be travelling through MacGregor territory. Toward the end of the day, Lamont and the MacGregors decided to go to a local inn, where they drank and ate together. A dispute arose, however, and Lamont stabbed and killed Alasdair's son. In the confusion, Lamont was able to escape, pursued by the MacGregors. Lamont eluded the MacGregors all night until, at break of day, he came upon Alasdair's house.

Not knowing who Alasdair was, Lamont asked for shelter and protection, and Alasdair agreed, taking Lamont in. Almost immediately, the MacGregors arrived and saw that Alasdair's guest was the same man who had murdered his son. They told Alasdair the truth, and pleaded with him to hand over Lamont, so that they could avenge his son's death.

But Alasdair refused. To allow vengeance would be to betray his promise, and hospitality was sacrosanct. Along with twelve armed MacGregors, he escorted his son's killer back to Lamont territory and let the man go.

Throughout the Highlands, it has always been known that no one can best the MacDonalds of Glen Coe at hospitality, not even the MacGregors. If you were away from home, and came to us, you would see our welcome. You would have nothing to fear. For however many days you needed shelter and food, you would have them. You would have whisky, a fire and a good bed, and perhaps, soon, our home would come to seem a bit less strange to you.

CHAPTER 11

1816

This nervous feeling came up in me as I looked around the yard. I started walking toward the house, reciting my speech: Hi, my name's Ryan Littrell, and I'm sorry to bother you, but I was doing some Internet research, and it said there was a cemetery here, I think it might be on your land, and I think one of my ancestors might be buried there.

But before I could get to the front door, a woman who looked to be in her forties opened the side door and stood without coming closer.

"May I help you?"

"Hi, my name's Ryan Littrell, and I'm sorry to bother you, but I was doing some Internet research, and it said there was a cemetery here, I think it might be on your land, and I think one of my ancestors might be buried there."

She looked down and paused, like she was saying to herself, well, OK. "And who's your ancestor?"

"A woman named Elizabeth McDonald, but I'm not completely sure she's my ancestor. I'm just pretty sure."

She nodded, as if the name rang a bell, and shut the door

behind her. She walked toward me and smiled. "My name's Judy Downing."

As we were shaking hands, I made the connection. "As in Ezekiel Downing?"

"That's right. Well, my married name is Collins, but Ezekiel Downing was my great-great-great-grandfather. He came here in 1816, and the land's been in our family since."

She invited me in. Her husband Bob would be home in a bit, she said. It was dinnertime, so I offered to come back some other day, but she would have none of it, and we started exchanging family stories. She told me about Ezekiel's days as a pioneer in Kentucky, how he died within a year of settling with his family here in Lincoln County, how her father had done a lot of research on the ancestry of Ezekiel and his wife Rachel Brown. Judy was descended from their son Ezekiel Downing, Jr., and her family had compiled a list of everyone buried in the cemetery, including Elizabeth McDonald.

Bob came home just then. He was glad to meet me, and chatted with Judy and me about the search for Hiram's ancestry. I told them why I suspected Elizabeth might be Hiram's mother, and then mentioned my attempt to visit Hiram and Nancy's grave down the road. "Oh, I know the man who owns that land," Judy said. "If you wanted, I could give him a call and see whether we can get in there while you're here."

The next thing I knew, she was dialing the phone. "Hello, Ron? This is Judy Collins, how are you doing? That's good. Yes, we're doing fine here, too. Listen, there's a man here I've been talking to who has some family members buried in that old cemetery down the road from us. Do you think if he and

I went down there, we'd be able to go in? That would be great. Oh, I see, OK, I'll make sure to close the gate when I leave. Thanks a lot, talk to you later." It turned out that the two ends of the lock could be pulled apart without a key or combination—it was only there to keep cows from getting through the gate.

Yes, I was about as smart as your average cow.

Because of the insects and the brush at the cemetery down the road, Judy would have to change clothes before taking me there, and Bob offered to go with me in the meantime to the cemetery behind their house. We went out the back door and made our way through the soybean field, row by row.

The cemetery was only about half the size of a tennis court, and Judy's list showed that only about fifty people were buried here. We went through the gate and looked around us: Old tombstones, covered with moss and dirt, some leaning over, some cracked to pieces. Weeds growing up over the stones. Judy's list said that Elizabeth was buried in the first row, which was probably this row here, the one closest to the gate. The stones were mostly illegible, but on this one, a thin and plain rectangular slab, I thought I could make out the letters "McD." We brushed off the moss and some of the soil, but the letters were faint from erosion.

Bob had an idea, though—rub some dirt over the inscription. I'd heard of people doing the same thing with flour, so why not? We shoveled some earth into our hands and took turns spreading it over the letters and brushing away the little clods until only a layer of dust remained. With every handful of dirt, a few more letters showed, so that the inscription appeared gradually, as when a photo is developing in a dark-room, and you can make out an eye at first and then the curve of a smile, and then the details fill in and a person fades into view. Her tombstone read:

IN
memory of
ELIZABETH
Consort of
Jno. McDONALD
BORN
Sep. 11, 1783
DIED
Nov. 16, 1853
Aged 70 years
2 mos. 5 days

"Consort" was simply another word for spouse, and it usually referred to a wife rather than a husband. We looked nearby for John's grave, but he wasn't buried here. That wasn't a surprise, though. Since Elizabeth was listed as the head of her household in Lincoln County in 1830, John probably died before then, somewhere. Still, why did Elizabeth move to Missouri after John's death?

As I was asking that question, Bob saw what looked like part of a tombstone sticking out from under a thin layer of soil next to Elizabeth's grave. When he brushed off the dirt, we could see that some time ago the tombstone had broken off at the bottom and was lying on the ground with its inscription facing up. It read: "Ezekiel D. McDonald, BORN May 24, 1815, DIED Jan. 14, 1859." He wasn't in any of the online transcriptions, and he must have been Elizabeth's son; not only was he buried next to her, but from the census records, I knew she was part of his household in 1850, toward the end of her life.

And that middle initial jumped out at me: Ezekiel *D.* McDonald. *Ezekiel Downing McDonald.* Elizabeth's son was named after the man who had owned this land—Ezekiel Downing, Sr., Judy's ancestor. Notice one other thing: Ezekiel McDonald was born in 1815, a year before Ezekiel Downing, Sr. migrated with his children to Missouri from Kentucky. So Elizabeth must have been in Kentucky by 1815, because she knew Ezekiel Downing, Sr. by then, and she knew him well enough to name one of her children after him.

There was one other grave I wanted to see. We found it not far from Elizabeth and Ezekiel. The carvings of angels on one of the four sides caught our eyes, but the stone had toppled over, breaking off from its base, and it was lying in weeds. Bob and I pulled it up from the ground, and brushed off the dirt and the insects until we saw her name: Eliza A. McDonald. Here was Eliza, daughter of Hiram and Liza Ann, and the opposite side of the same stone gave the name of Mary A. Tilford.

Eliza Ann had been buried next to her aunt Mary, her mother Liza Ann's sister, but no one else from the Tilford family was here, and I wondered why, out loud. Bob said he didn't know, but anyway he thought he'd try to find a way to put this stone back up to where it was supposed to be. We tried to balance it on top of the base that it had been separated from, but it wouldn't stay. So we had to settle for leaning it up against the base. We looked down at it, and Bob looked at me, and I looked at Bob, and we decided our quick fix was good enough for now.

As we walked back to the house, Bob said he planned on taking the time to clear the weeds and refurbish the tombstones soon. I turned around to take one more look at the cemetery—the little circle of trees and moss covered tombstones out in the middle of the soybean field. Crickets were chirping now, and there was the humidity on my skin and the itch of new mosquito bites. The sun was back, and it had warmed up a bit even though evening was approaching.

Back inside the house, Judy was ready for the Bryant Creek Cemetery: Thick overalls and heavy boots. As she and I walked toward her truck, she said all her siblings and cousins had moved away, so she was the only descendant of Ezekiel Downing, Sr. still living on the land that he bought back in 1816. Heading down the road, I told her about my moves, from my childhood in Chatham to college near Chicago to law school near Boston to my job in New York. I was about to tell her I sometimes wished I hadn't moved around so much, but we were already there, pulling off to the side of the road in front of the gate.

The lock opened easily, and it was only a few more steps to the cluster of old tombstones sitting in the tree shade. Judy said she'd always thought about visiting this cemetery, but never had. The undergrowth was thick, and where there was grass, it hadn't been mowed for some time. As I looked up and around, the sun shimmered here and there through the branches and leaves. I looked down and began scanning the tombstones, but then I didn't have to, because I could see that familiar name. Their tombstone was under a tree, right at the cemetery entrance. A single flower was etched in the upper left corner, and the inscription read:

H & N McDONALD
BORN NOV. 12, 1806
DIED OCT. 27, 1882
BORN DEC. 16, 1818
DIED JUNE 17, 1910

The first set of dates was for Hiram, the second set for Nancy. Notice, Judy said, how new the tombstone is, compared to its base. The original tombstone had been replaced by a smooth, marble one. The thought occurred to us that some unknown cousin of my great-grandpa Lee, another descendant of Hiram and Nancy, must have had the new stone placed here, maybe because the old one had eroded or cracked.

Judy walked off to look at other graves, and I turned my eyes from Hiram and Nancy's gravestone to the ground in front of it. I reached down and touched the soil, and felt the grass growing up. There was quiet all around.

On the drive back to the house, where my car was waiting, I figured that my visit was coming to a close, and thanked Judy for all her help. Sure, she said, but she was wondering about something.

Elizabeth McDonald, Eliza Ann McDonald, and Mary A. Tilford had always stood out in her mind, she said, because she knew that everyone else who was buried in the cemetery was descended from Ezekiel Downing, Sr., or at least was a spouse or in-law of one of his descendants. She asked me whether I had time to come back in for a minute, and I took her up on the offer and followed her back in.

After saying hello to Bob and giving him an overview of what we'd seen, Judy went back into her office and came back with a bundle of papers. We sat for a while, going through copies of old wills and family letters, but there was nothing about Elizabeth or Eliza to be found. After a while, we came across a bundle of documents that her father had put together, compiling the family's records and setting out the results of his searches.

"I've looked through this before," Judy said as she flipped through it, almost like she was shuffling a deck of cards. But then I thought I saw that familiar name again. When she turned back to the page, we found a list of the known children of Ezekiel Downing, Sr. The fourth one down was Elizabeth Downing, "Died 1853, Consort of John McDonald."

It all came together. Ezekiel Downing McDonald, Elizabeth's son, was named after Ezekiel Downing, Sr. because he was Elizabeth's father, Ezekiel's grandfather. It was no coincidence that after her husband John died, Elizabeth and her children came to Lincoln County out of hundreds of counties in the United States. This is where her family already was. And now it made perfect sense that Eliza Ann, Hiram's daughter, had been buried here. As Judy had said, everyone who was buried in this cemetery was a descendant of Ezekiel Downing, Sr., or at least was a spouse or in-law of a descendant. Eliza Ann was here because she was a Downing—*on her father Hiram's side*.

That's when Judy and I looked at each other and realized we were cousins.

We sat for a while longer as the sunlight dimmed, and we talked about our family, about what their lives might have been like, about what we could do to uncover more. Those things weren't on my mind, though, as Judy and Bob and I exchanged phone numbers and email addresses, as we said goodbye, as I got in the car and headed back to my hotel.

Because I just wanted to go back, now that I knew. I wanted to go up to Elizabeth's grave. I would brush away all the dirt and make sure it wasn't going to fall down, and then I would look around for a flower to place there. I would say: I know you never met me, and I know you don't know my name, but I am from you, and I just wish you could see me. I wish you could see that someone knows who you were and what you did, and I won't let anybody forget you, not ever again.

CHAPTER 12

A' GHÀIDHEALTACHD

Tha fhios agam nach bi ' nur cinn ach am fèileadh agus a'
phìob-mhòr nuair a smaoinicheas sibh oirnn.

I know that when you think of us, you only see kilts and
bagpipes in your head.

But it has always been the less performed ways, the nods
and understandings from the cradle, that have fastened us together, and these have reached far beyond my own glen. When
I speak, for instance, of how Glen Coe people always took in
strangers, I am speaking of something that has dwelled in all
of the Gaels, throughout all of the Highlands and all of the
Western Isles, not just here beneath the Three Sisters.

This you will hear in the old saying: *Bheirinn cuid-oidhche*
dha ged a bhiodh ceann fir fo 'achlais. (I would give him food
and lodging for the night even if he had a man's head under
his arm.) Our ancestors knew that giving begat giving, that
care begat care, and thus they said: *Gus an tràighear a' mhuir*
le cliabh, cha bhi fear fial falamh. (Until the ocean is emptied
with a basket, the generous man will never be empty-handed.)

They knew that there was no shame in coming to your

fellow clansmen and clanswomen for help, so long as it was needed. No, the only shame was for those who turned a blind eye, because any of us, even the strongest, would one day face struggle, and even the weakest could one day regain their force. Nearly everyone saw this truth, and passed it on to their children and to their grandchildren: *Beathaich thusa mise an-diugh agus beathaichidh mise thusa a-màireach.* (Feed me today and I'll feed you tomorrow.)

There were many times, even, when the hungry but strong ones gave themselves up to the past and the future, because they kept in mind what they knew: *Dà rud nach còir a bhith falamh: goile an t-seann duine agus làmh an leanaibh bhig.* (Two things that should not be empty: the stomach of the old and the hand of the child.)

It was for this reason that the greatest of them were those who gave the most. All people expected their clan's chief to provide for anyone who needed help, and he would be praised accordingly. The most honourable chief was the one who followed the ancient custom of *bord follaiseach*, inviting clanspeople in need to come into his home and eat at his table for a year and a day. For the chief was a father, not a despot. His people were not serfs or peasants, but fellow clansmen and clanswomen. Only because they fought for him, only because their fields and cattle gave him sustenance, could he hold any power at all.

Thus they reminded him: *Far nach bi nì, caillidh an rìgh a chòir.* (A king will lose his rights where there is no wealth.) Women and men alike took pride in their chief only because he merited it, because he and his ancestors had stood, always, with a honed blade, and had defended them without backing down. All of them understood this: *Is àirde tuathanach air a chasan na duine-uasal air a ghlùinean.* (A common person standing on his feet is taller than a nobleman on his knees.)

You might hear me speak of battle, and perhaps think my people bloodthirsty, but my ancestors did not fight for the sake of power or lands alone. They fought, too, because their chief, their clan, and their home were worthy of being made known. Their chief's courage, his generosity, reflected upon them because he was one of them, who inherited the same bounded soil, and loved the same mountains against the sky.

That is why every sword's arc was also a speaking. Their sprinting charge told of what was in them. Conquering for the sake of conquering was unseemly; only those with cramped spirits could covet yet more fields of pigs and barley. A chief already had enough snow peaks and salmon-flecked rivers. No, it was far better to die for your people on the battlefield, and be remembered, than to live in fat splendour until you expired, sleeping as ever, in a bed. All Highlanders knew: *Is buaine bladh na saoghal.* (Fame is more lasting than life.)

Fame, however, only came to those of great honour, and honour only came to those with the daring to defeat the powerful. The greatest shame came to those who preyed upon the powerless: *Is mairg a chuireadh farran air fann.* (Woe to him who bothers the weak.) A true man did not attack needlessly, but once a foe worthy of him appeared, he would relent only with his life. An inscription upon a sword read: *Na tarraing mi gun adhbhar, is na pill mi gun chliù.* (Do not draw me without a reason, and do not return me without honour.)

94

The great man ensured, too, that his clanspeople would remain with their land, always. Under our Gaelic law, a family had the right to remain on their land once they had lived there for three generations, for here was their *dùthchas*. Here was their heritage, their inheritance. Their land could no more be taken from them than could their memories be plucked from their minds. Their homes could no more be stolen from them than could their ancestors' blood be removed from their veins.

Clanspeople lived by their bonds to their neighbours, who were always their cousins, because their shared ancestors had brought them together for the rest of their days: *Cha nigh na tha de uisge anns a' mhuir ar càirdeas.* (All of the water in the ocean could not wash away our kinship.) In all things, they remembered: *Cha duine, duine 'na aonar.* (A person by himself is not a person.) They belonged together in one place, generation after generation, for home does not speak the fleeting language of money.

This, above all, has always puzzled the English. I do not mean to say that Englishmen know little of manners or family, but we have often noticed something rather lurking behind their comportment. There may be a quick, studying glance at the silver, just as a witticism first brings laughter all about the table. There may be hints embedded within questions, helpfully suggesting that the conversation turn toward matters of business. If such matters are not raised directly, one might encounter certain pleasant subterfuges, as another's wealth is obliquely referenced while everyone pretends, naturally, to be embarrassed by the mere thought of it.

Our understanding of wealth is found in the story of

my cousin Alasdair MacDonald, chief of the MacDonalds of Keppoch. Once, Alasdair was in London at an elegant dinner, attended by a number of titled gentlemen, surrounded by all of the blaring signals of muted opulence. The host, at one point, spoke of the silver candleholders sitting at his table, and gently remarked upon their great value. Alasdair was loath to give even the slightest offence to his host, but soon heard one of his fellow guests speak insultingly of the Highlands, and of Highland people.

He looked about the table and said to all of them, "I could show you a dozen candleholders in my home that are far more valuable than these." The Englishmen were in disbelief, quite sure that the Highlands were barbarous and deprived, and so they bet Alasdair a large sum of money that his twelve candleholders could not measure up to those of their host. Alasdair invited the host up to Keppoch, where he could see the proof.

Several weeks later, the host came with his friend, a fellow Englishman, to Alasdair's home, and Alasdair greeted them at his door with much warmth. The Englishmen had expected a great castle, but they found a home that was modest, by their standards. To the table were brought the bounty of the clan's lands; the guests were handed venison from the peak of *Beinn a' Bhric*, salmon from the river of Orchy, the freshest fruits, and strong whisky. Although the visitors enjoyed the food and drink, Alasdair noticed that they were eyeing his possessions. At this, he made a motion, and twelve of his best men appeared. Each of them held a torch in his left hand, a sword in his right.

Alasdair looked at his guests and said: "You now see the

candleholders of Keppoch, and I would ask you without any hesitation if there is enough gold and silver in all of England that could possibly buy them." The guests saw that they had lost the bet, but Alasdair refused to take their money. Instead, he offered a toast to their health, and offered them full hospitality in his home for as long as they wished. They stayed with him for another week, enjoying his family's smiles and tales, his bard's poetry, and his piper's songs.

Those guests, as well as many of the Lowlanders within our own country, would be surprised to learn one truth, as they have exerted so much effort in the forgetting of it. That truth is this: For many centuries, our Gaelic hearth was the heart of Scotland, and we were at home in this land long before English ways came to us.

Yet, even to this day, the English and the Lowlanders have disdained us. We have had our centuries of poetry, our ancient and respected laws, our engraved intricacies, and the reaching of our music, but they have always indicted us as savages. Their customs alone, their beliefs and their language alone, are to be considered civilised.

Our ancestors brought Christianity to Scotland, but we held to many of the old ways of the Church, and so they called us heathens. Their princes never wearied of warfare, of pillage, and yet they looked to our clan battles and pronounced us murderous. They made their people into serfs, but said that clanship was primitive. They took so much land through conquest, they grabbed so much land through lawyers, and now they have even colonised much of the world, but when they heard of a Highland foray, they called us thieves.

One of them wrote that we are "a savage and untamed nation, rude and independent, given to rapine, easy living, of a docile and warm disposition, comely in person but unsightly in dress...and exceedingly cruel." A Lowland, Scottish king charitably divided us into two classes: "I shortly comprehend them all in two sorts of people: the one that dwelleth in our mainland, that are barbarous for the most part, and yet mixed with some show of civility: the other, that dwelleth in the Isles and are all utterly barbarous, without any sort or show of civility."

Another one wrote of us: "The Highlanders of Scotland are a sort of wretches that have no other consideration of honour, friendship, obedience or government...." Helpful churchmen of Glasgow have ventured that we "might yet become a noble accession to the Commonwealth," but only if we are "brought to Religion, Humanity, Industry, and the Low Country Language." The MacDonalds of Glen Coe, in particular, are "at a distance from politeness, and like many other rebels, drowned in ignorance."

Lying behind this sneer, behind this contented derision, has always been the force we call *Mi-run mor nan Gall*.

The Lowlanders' Great Hatred.

CHAPTER 13

W.D. AND
GEORGE ANNIE

I reached into my bag for the one book I'd brought along to Missouri. It was called *Glencoe*, with a cover that said: "The terrible story of the Highland Massacre." On the front were two men in kilts, their backs to me. Their kilts showed the same tartan, green and dark blue, and one of them was holding a sword and shield. Over their shoulders, I could see what they were seeing, off in the distance: Flames and rising smoke. They were looking out from behind a few large rocks, with snow on the ground all around them.

Now I was one step closer. By discovering Hiram's mother, I'd also discovered his father, and so my McDonald family tree had a new generation, there at the top:

John McDonald, m. Elizabeth Downing
|
Hiram McDonald (1806-1882), m. Nancy Buchanan
|
William Duncan McDonald (1855-1935), m. Georgianna Wilson
|
Will McDonald (1875-1964), m. Linnie Hagan

|
Lee McDonald (my great-grandpa), m. Mary Bridgewater
|
Betty McDonald (my grandma), m. Don McCord

Judy and I had spent so much time talking last night that I'd had trouble finding a place still serving dinner. One decent night's sleep later, I was sitting in the restaurant at my hotel, not far from the courthouse in Troy, and I finished up my cereal, refilled my cup of coffee.

The book I was reading, along with a few Internet sites, told me that the MacDonalds of Glencoe were also known as MacIains, after their first chief. For generations, the Glencoe chiefs took the name, and the English version of Iain was John. So Hiram's father John might have been named after his Glencoe ancestors.

Then again, John might have gotten his name because his family had already been Americanized, Anglicized. Maybe his parents named him John just because it was a common name on this side of the ocean. Certainly by the time John and Elizabeth were having children, in the early 1800s, the family wasn't interested in Gaelic names, and maybe was opposed to them. Just look at Hiram's siblings: Cyrus, Betsy, Rebecca, Darius, Thomas, James, Patsy, Nancy, and Ezekiel.

Glencoe had been lost, too. My great-grandpa Lee, who'd been with me for all those hours, had probably never heard the word. So where on the family tree had the knowing been cut? Was it John who decided that the story was no longer worth telling, or was it his children, or was it closer to me, people I knew? And whoever it was, what made them think the story deserved forgetting?

Maybe these things would show themselves once I uncovered John and his family, his brothers and sisters and parents. But for now, this morning, they were a mystery. All I knew for sure was that, sometime before 1830, Elizabeth came here to Lincoln County, Missouri with her children. It seemed likely that John had died before Elizabeth and the children made this move, but I couldn't forget the possibility that there was something more going on—maybe Elizabeth and the children left for Missouri even though John was alive and well. Either way, it was clear that Hiram and his siblings went to be with his mother Elizabeth's family, rather than with his father John's.

If I were going to uncover what happened to John, if I were going to uncover his family's history, I'd have to look beyond Missouri. I'd have to search for the state and county where he and Elizabeth lived before the move. It appeared that they'd been somewhere in Kentucky, but how could I find the exact place? Where was I supposed to look?

In the weeks before my trip, I'd already started asking these questions. Online, I'd been fishing for facts about the men and women I suspected were Hiram's siblings, because even though I hadn't found any hints about Hiram's pre-Missouri life, I'd been hoping there were records about one of his brothers or sisters. I'd looked, and looked some more, but hadn't had luck with any of them. Except for one.

Typing in Cyrus' name at Ancestry.com, I'd found a family tree that had been contributed by one of his descendants. It listed his wife and then the place where they'd been married:

Warren County, Kentucky. It made sense that Cyrus got married before the family came to Missouri, since the 1830 Lincoln County, Missouri census showed Cyrus and Elizabeth as the only heads of household with the McDonald name.

I'd been keeping this Warren County, Kentucky allegation in the back of my mind, not wanting to get ahead of myself. But that was before yesterday, before going to Judy's house. Now that I knew Hiram was the son of Elizabeth and John, I could say, with near certainty, that he was the brother of Cyrus. And if they *were* brothers, and if this family tree at Ancestry.com were true, then Hiram must have been in or near Warren County at some time before 1830. Perhaps that's where John's family lived, and where John passed away.

I could see my next step—searching for records in one wooded, hilly county in southern Kentucky.

For now, though, I was finishing up breakfast at my hotel and glancing at newspaper headlines. Glancing, rather than reading, because my mind was on something else. I saw Elizabeth's gravestone again, almost as I'd seen it yesterday afternoon, behind Judy's house. The inscription on the gravestone had told me: Here lies Elizabeth Downing McDonald. The remains of her body were right there, just below where I was standing. This wasn't *about* her; it *was* her. Against that concreteness, a record or a picture has the consistency of air.

Among the chances never given to Elizabeth was this one chance to be next to John again. There couldn't be a gravestone inscribed with the easy phrase "John and Elizabeth McDonald," because his body was away. His name had to stand in for his body.

And see how his name defined her: She was called "Elizabeth, Consort of Jno. McDonald." In the tiny space allotted to her life story, her gravestone didn't tell us what kind of mother or grandmother she was, or whether she was uncommonly devoted to God or whether she was admired for her integrity, and it said nothing about the toughness and courage she must have shown. Her identity as John's wife seemed to take precedence over all of the other things that she was.

But what I knew about Elizabeth didn't suggest that she was submissive. She moved her family to Missouri without getting remarried, raised several children on her own, ran a working farm without a husband, and even bought land in her own name when she was in her sixties. Besides, it wasn't as though she'd been compelled to have John's name on her gravestone; in the two cemeteries I visited, there were several married women whose gravestones didn't give their husbands' names. No, the inscription probably read "Consort of Jno. McDonald" because Elizabeth *wanted* it to—or because her children knew that's what she would have wanted.

She understood, of course, what was at stake in letting herself be seen in this light: Once you're defined via another, your once-independent territories aren't just yours, but also, partly, theirs.

So it's no accident that two people who've been together for years might say, "We *belong* together," just as it's no accident that a person might say of her lifelong home, "I *belong* here." Belonging is always *belonging to*, a little surrender to the person we belong with, or a little surrender to the place where we belong. Belonging isn't the same as possession, because belonging always involves surrender, while possession never does. Possession is one-sided: The possessor doesn't give up even an ounce of himself to the thing that he possesses.

That's why we don't belong in a place just by possessing it. If we belong there, it's not only because we can lay a claim on the place, but also because the place can lay a claim on *us*. The place we call home isn't so much the place that's given itself up to us; it's the place we've given ourselves up to. And the same is true for two people: They belong together only because each has given up to the other, so much that it can no longer be taken back. It's only through loss that we belong.

On the day Elizabeth was buried, when her death was still young, memories of her belonging weren't yet remote. Here was her son Hiram, and Hiram's wife Nancy, my great-grandpa Lee's great-grandparents. Standing near Hiram were his brothers and sisters, and Elizabeth's brothers and sisters, and her in-laws and her grandchildren and her nieces and nephews. Even from here, I can make out the creases in their skin that must have come from years working in the fields, and the calluses and the black dresses and the strong hands and some downward eyes that said, Thy will be done, on earth as it is in heaven. And as Hiram walked away from the burial, he must have known that his mother and father were in him, and that they would stay in him, and that they would always belong there.

Down the road, and about 150 years later, I was at my hotel, finishing my coffee and looking again at my map. It was approaching check-out time, and I figured I'd be back on the road to Chatham, to central Illinois, by lunchtime. I'd be in New York the day after tomorrow, and then I'd begin my Warren County, Kentucky search. But today, here, there was one more thing I needed to see.

I got in the car and headed out of Troy. It was clearer today, a little warmer, and the air already felt humid. Wooden stands on the side of the road were selling fruit and fireworks. I came to the state highway, like yesterday, but this time I kept driving, and soon I was in Pike County, where my great-great-great-grandpa William Duncan lived, where Great-grandpa Lee was born. New housing developments were being built next to cornfields, and ranch houses had long driveways. Barns were off in the horizon, on both sides, and just after the town of Bowling Green, I turned left onto Highway 54. I was on my way to Vandalia, where Great-grandpa Lee lived before moving to my hometown Chatham when he was a teenager.

This stretch was like the country roads around Chatham—flatter than the places around Troy, with more farmers' fields and more heat, and always that sky. And when I came into Vandalia, I could see how Great-grandpa Lee might have convinced himself that he could be at home in that new place in Illinois. Because the houses here were almost the same as in Chatham, and so was the layout of the town and the grass in the lawns and the signs and the front porches, and how some of the trees on opposite sides of the street would come dangerously close to meeting one another, up above me as I drove, but never quite met halfway.

I got onto Main Street and followed it north out of town for a few moments, until I could see the cemetery to my right, surrounded by fields. Pulling in and stopping the car on the side of the road, I had that dismal what-have-I-gotten-myself-into feeling. The cemetery was a lot bigger than expected. The gravestones took up several football fields, lined up in long, neat rows on green grass.

Well, I hadn't come all the way from central Illinois to quit now. Before getting out of the car, I pulled out a picture I'd brought along.

Mom and Aunt Donna had found it in the same old box that contained the anonymous letter. The picture is of my great-great-great-grandpa William Duncan, standing alone in front of a house, right before the front porch. He looks like he's in his 70s, after his wife Anna died. The house is probably his, here in Vandalia, the house he and Anna lived in together. His shoulders are narrow, his hair is bright white, he has a drooping bushy mustache, as white as his hair. The shirt's buttoned all the way up under his wool overcoat, and you can see the wrinkles and veins on his hands.

I brought the picture up close. Words can't catch what's happening in a picture, but his eyes seemed to be saying: I know who I am, and I'll take care of myself, and it doesn't matter to me whether you like it or not.

This picture of William Duncan made me think of one other thing. In that mystery box, Mom and Aunt Donna had discovered an envelope from him, addressed to Great-grandpa Lee and Great-grandma Mary. This was in 1927, seven years after William Duncan's wife Anna had passed away. Inside was a card congratulating them on the birth of their first child, and on the back of the card, William Duncan had written just one word: "Grandpa."

I put away the picture and got out of the car. I started in one corner of the cemetery, scanning the names on the stones as I walked down one row of graves, then the next row, and then the next. The names kept coming as I walked down the rows, and they instantly passed away, the way a face in a city is forgotten the moment you walk by it. Reading all the names like this felt disrespectful, to be registering them so fast and moving on. Flowers had been placed on some of the graves, fresh or wilted or plastic. Many of the newer graves had them, but the older graves had few, and the oldest had none.

After about five minutes of walking along and scanning names, no luck. And after about ten minutes, still no luck. The sun was beating down harder now. As I walked along, I came across some names I recognized. Linnie's maiden name, Hagan. Anna's mom's maiden name, Houston. Thomas J. Buchanan, born 1861, probably Nancy's nephew. And a lot of McDonalds—Arch B. and J. Mae, Lillian, Leslie and Velma. I took pictures of these maybe-cousins as I came across them, but the battery on the camera was running low, and I didn't have a charger.

Then, after a few more minutes of looking, I found it. Even though people called her Anna or Annie, her full name was Georgianna, and the gravestone read:

McDONALD
W.D.
AUG. 13, 1855-JUNE 18, 1935
GEORGE ANNIE HIS WIFE
NOV. 12, 1854-AUG. 4. 1920

The camera came on. I rushed to get one last shot, and

got it, and then the power went off for good.

I looked around. Flat land to the horizon, acres of graves, a car driving by in the distance every once in a while. Nobody else was around, the wind wasn't blowing. Should have brought some flowers along.

I bent down and ran my hands over the blades of grass. I reached over and touched their stone, and kept my hand there for a few seconds. Hello, my name is Ryan, and I'm your great-great-great-grandson.

I stood back up and looked down at those two end dates: August 4, 1920 for her, and June 18, 1935 for him. He had almost fifteen years of living alone in their house, fifteen years of posing for pictures on his own. Fifteen years of signing cards that just said, "Grandpa." Maybe he'd already caught glimpses of aloneness before he was ever alone, because he'd seen his mom Nancy live for twenty-eight years after his dad Hiram passed away.

But he and Anna never had *me* in their thoughts. They never knew that one day, some mystery great-great-great-grandson would be told about an old letter and then go on a road trip to Missouri. They never knew that this distant grandson would fall for someone, and get married far away. And so they never knew that I could imagine what it might be like to be the one who someday writes:

> Since you left, I'll be at home and I'll drive the car and I'll watch TV and I'll try to fall asleep, but half the time I have to keep saying to myself: It's natural, let it be, this is the way it goes, should have seen

it coming, this is the way it is, this is the way it is. *This is the way it is.*

But everybody else, out there, they don't see any of that. Here's what they see: Old guy, alone, wrinkles, slow walk, clothes a little out of fashion but he doesn't care, and he says something funny every once in a while. That's when their smile comes on, the practiced one, the dismissive, nice one. It always happens in that restaurant I've been going to. I walk in, and the lady does her nice hello, and calls me honey, just like she says hello and gives her honey-greeting to all the other folks coming in early for dinner. And the next day, she says exactly the same thing, and smiles exactly the same way. Like I'm some little kid. Like I can't tell what's going on around me.

The grandkids still come up and give me a hug, and the little one still gives me a kiss, the way you always liked. But the older ones look at me sometimes like they don't exactly know how to deal with me anymore. I know they still feel the same way about me, obviously, but they always act like they just don't want to offend.

The kids try to help, and you know I love them for it, but they're just so sure of themselves whenever they talk about us. They say I'm mourning your absence. They say I'm "searching for closure." One of them mentioned a good doctor, and another one got me some book about chicken soup. But you and I know that it's not about your absence at all. It's about your closeness. And if they understood a single damn thing, it might be worth telling them that sometimes, when I'm sitting here, I ask you: Why won't you let me be? But there's no point in talking about it, since I already know why you won't let me be: It's because I don't *want* you to let me be.

Because I know you remember that day, when I was so nervous and you almost laughed for a second because my hands were so cold, and we said *'til death do us part.* It was easy enough to say those words, and then all the years afterwards, when things were tough sometimes, you know I always came around: *'Til death do us part* meant that I wouldn't ever give up on this. And I didn't. I understood it, I got it, I was on board, I wasn't going to complain too much.

So maybe I never said this, but there were times when I'd wake up at night, and I could tell that you were lying next to me, but I couldn't hear your breath. I'd start wondering, then I'd start getting a little worried. Then I'd say to myself, Don't be an idiot, she's fine, you know she's fine. And anyway, it's not like I really thought something was wrong—I was just wondering, I was thinking it might be a possibility, in the back of my head. So I'd inch over, and then lean in, quiet as I could, and I'd listen in, and soon I'd hear that regular exhaling and inhaling, and then I'd feel the slight movement pressing up against the sheets.

Now, though, there's nothing when I wake up in the night. It's just the walls, and the dark. OK, stop with the heart beating so fast. Just calm down. This is the way it is, this is the way it goes, it's natural, this is the way it is.

But maybe you didn't know about how the water draped down your skin when you were in the shower. How I could tell your scent as soon as you came up to me. How my hands would get caught in your spider web hair, and I never really minded being helpless. How you kept all of us going. How we'd be at a party, and you'd laugh that one way, and everybody else just thought it was a regular laugh, but I knew exactly what it meant.

And maybe some of this was already there when I was a kid, on that day when Great-grandpa Lee was standing alone in his dark suit and tie. I wanted to go up to him and help him, and tell him I thought he might be OK someday, but there was nothing I could do. He was standing next to her, surrounded by the flowers and her coffin and the condolence cards, as the last of the mourners walked out, saying they'd be at the funeral tomorrow.

We were still here, though, his children and grandchildren and great-grandchildren. And now the funeral home was silent around us. The chairs, all lined up in rows, were empty. The employees were leaving the room. But he was still standing, the grandson of William Duncan and Anna, the great-grandson of Hiram and Nancy, the great-great-grandson of John and Elizabeth. He looked down at her for a few more seconds, and didn't say anything. Then he leaned down, kissed her, and said, "Goodbye, buddy."

Chapter 14

Dál Riata

*Leis gu bheil beagan eòlais agaibh oirnn a-nis, leigibh leam
ar sgeul innse dhuibh.*

Now that you know something about us, let me tell you
our story.

It is a story, not a mere moment, because the scourges
did not happen in the way that lightning strikes, or as a hawk
swoops. They did not appear with a line of alien soldiers
blocking the sun of a sudden. No, they came with the usurpers, whose advance needed centuries, not months or years.
They came with the rise of the false clan, who served foreign
masters again and again, decade after decade, mountain after
new mountain. They came, as well, with the Englishmen's hatred, which began small, but over generations grew.

Perhaps the English hate us because they know that our
ancestors were Irish. They know that our ancestors long ago
brought the Irish tongue and Irish ways to Britain, to the island which they will always consider to be theirs alone. We are
descended from Conn Cétchathach, Conn of the Hundred
Battles, who was High King of Ireland 120 years after the

birth of Christ. More than a millennium after Conn's death, the warriors of Clan Donald would still hear these words: *A Chlanna Cuinn cuimhnichibh | Cruas an am na h-iorghaile.* (Children of Conn, remember hardihood in the time of battle.)

Our ancestors left Ireland and came to the Highlands and Isles of Scotland in the fifth century, founding the kingdom of Dál Riata, which spanned the northwest of Scotland and part of northern Ireland. Perhaps this union, across so many shores, seems odd to many of you, whose eyes are accustomed to viewing Ireland and Scotland as different countries. Yet our ancestors' maps were centred upon the waters between the two lands, upon the isles lying there. They could sail from one isle to the next in merely a few hours, and could go from an Irish port to a Scottish mooring in less than a day, for the two lands are less than twenty miles from one another at their shortest remove.

Across these different soils, across horizons of waves, the Gaels made a home, and from them comes each of our ways. From them comes each carved curve in us.

We Gaels unified with the Picts, our fellow Celts who had long inhabited all of the northern places, and together formed the kingdom of Alba. By the middle of the eleventh century, the kings of Alba had conquered the Anglo-Saxons to our south, so that the Highlands and Isles in the north and the Lowlands in the south were now one kingdom. Here Gaelic was spoken, not only in the Highlands and Isles, but also at the royal court and in much of the Lowlands. The Romans had always referred to the Irish as the *Scoti*, and so this kingdom of the Gaels came to be called Scotland.

For all that, most of the Lowlanders in the south of our country continued to speak their variant of English, and our Gaelic ways did not become theirs. Ensconced down in the south, the Scottish kings began to retreat from the language and character of their ancestors, speaking English with greater and more accomplished fluency and marrying English royalty. They gained lands in England and spent more and more of their time there. Soon, the whole of the southern half of Scotland was being Anglicised, with feudal lords in the place of clan chiefs, and with tenants in the place of clansmen and clanswomen.

But in the twelfth century, a man called *Somhairle* rose up in the Highlands and the Isles to challenge the Lowland, Scottish king. In your language he is known as Somerled, and like the king, he came from the line of the sovereigns of Dál Riata. He came of age at a time when many of our lands were ruled, not by the king, but by Vikings, who had invaded and remained.

Although of royal blood, Somerled was not born a king's son; he was chosen to lead by the local clans, and presently vindicated their trust with a victory over the Norse king. So complete was Somerled's conquest that the Vikings never again would rule our lands. The Lowland king knew better than to advance upon united Highlanders, and in the year 1160, he signed a treaty accepting Somerled's lordship over most of the Isles and much of the Highlands.

Now the descendants of Dál Riata had their own land, ruled by their own people, in their own ways. This is the land where peaks stand high, misted, just above the pulling away of the waves, and the hills slope up, green, from the still of the lochs. Here the beaches rise quickly to become meadows, and the meadows rise quickly into mountains. Like so many, I speak of Somerled, and remain in remembrance of him, because he was the founder of this Gaelic kingdom, independent from both Scotland and England, which would live for centuries.

Yet we speak of Somerled not only because he did so much to form our Gaelic moat. We speak of him, too, because he was the founder of the Clan Donald. His descendants were the MacDonald chiefs, and they succeeded him as sovereigns of the kingdom. His son Ranald was esteemed for his piety, and built up the church and monasteries upon the Isle of Iona, while his grandson Donald, who gave the clan its name, was a commanding warrior, resisting the Lowland king at every turn.

In the early 14th century, however, when Donald's grandson Angus Og was Lord of the Isles, the MacDonalds united with Lowlanders, who had produced a king worthy of following into battle. His name was Robert the Bruce, and though his father came from a line of Normans and Englishmen, his mother was Celtic, from the west, and he was raised speaking the Gaelic language. When Robert was still a young man, the English king, Edward I, claimed lordship over Scotland, planting English soldiers, nobles and sheriffs upon Scottish soil, and torturing and executing the hero William Wallace.

In 1306, only seven months after Wallace's beheading, Robert was crowned King of Scotland, and it was he who felt the first unglanced stings: Only a few months after being crowned, he and his army were routed by the English, and he was forced to flee. The English executed his brother Neil. They captured his wife and queen, Elizabeth, his daughter Marjorie and his sister Christina. They took his sister Mary and placed her in an outdoor cage for all the public to see, and would keep her there for four years.

Nearly alone, sought by English assassins and spies, Robert escaped to the west, where he came upon the MacDonald stronghold of Saddell Castle and was welcomed by our Angus Og. The MacDonald took in Robert and gave him protection, spiriting him to one of our isles off of the coast of Ireland.

Once his strength returned to him, Robert returned to Scotland, newly armed with Islesmen. Now began his rise: For the next several years, he and his men proceeded from victory to victory, defeating much larger English armies and vanquishing those Scots who had risen against him. By March of 1314, almost all of Scotland was under his power, and so a massive English force moved north, led by Edward II, son of the recently deceased Edward I. On the 23rd of June, Robert and his united Scots met Edward's army at Bannockburn.

It was on the second day of the battle, at the moment when English knights first began their fear, that Robert turned to Angus Og and asked him to bring in his MacDonalds, upon the right line. As the Highlanders moved forward, and saw their charge lying before them, Robert told Angus Og, "My hope is constant in thee."

The MacDonalds ran with their swords and axes. There were so many of the Anglo-Saxons, so many more Englishmen than Scots, and yet the men of the Isles wrecked them, sent them. Our Lowland allies, too, brought spears and swords through English armour, and their cuts and thrusts said: Leave my country. Be gone.

When Edward fled the field, the whole of the English army fled behind him, and though England would not formally recognise it for several years, Scotland became independent on that battlefield. In recognition of the MacDonalds' deeds, Robert declared that, henceforth, the men of Clan Donald would always be given the honoured place on the right wing of any Scottish army. As a further testament to his gratitude, Robert granted Angus Og MacDonald lands in the Highlands and Isles that once had belonged to Highlanders opposing Robert.

So it was that the MacDonalds came to Glen Coe.

For the glen was among those lands given to Angus Og, and he soon granted it to his son *Iain Fraoch*, Iain of the Heather, who became our first chief. Since the time of Iain, we have known ourselves as the MacIains of Glen Coe, wearing sprigs of heather in memory of our ancestor. For those of us who still make note of such things, the heather that grows all about the glen reminds us of him. It reminds us of the ancestors who wore it.

Before the MacDonalds, people called MacEanruig lived here, and a number live here still. In English, today, they are usually called Henderson, or MacHenry, or MacKendrick. Iain Fraoch was himself of MacEanruig blood; his mother was the daughter of Dugall MacEanruig, the leader of the MacEanruigs of Glen Coe. The MacEanruigs accepted Iain

Fraoch as their chief, and in their honour, they have been the hereditary pipers of our clan ever since. Whenever we looked across to an enemy, whenever the MacIain chief returned to the glen from a journey, whenever one of us crossed to the burial isle for the final time, the music came in a MacEanruig's breath.

Of course, Iain Fraoch's father Angus Og was not the only chief to fight with Robert the Bruce, and the MacDonalds were not the only clan to gain from the victory at Bannockburn. One family, in particular, prospered much.

They were descended from a 13th century man named Gillespic, who lived in Clackmannanshire, in the Lowlands. Though Gillespic's ancestry is not clear, it is thought that he did not come from the Gaels of the Highlands and Isles, but from those other Celts who had long inhabited the Lowlands around Glasgow, to the south of us, before the Anglo-Saxons invaded. Only later did Gillespic's family come farther north and west, to Loch Awe at the southern tip of the Highlands, and even then, many of their lands and castles were in the English-speaking Lowlands. For generations after Gillespic, a nickname remained with them: "Crooked mouth." This nickname, in Gaelic, is *cam beul*, and so they came to be called Campbell.

It was Neill Campbell, Gillespic's grandson, who steadfastly served Robert the Bruce, receiving yet more lands as his reward. His service to Robert, in fact, served as the guiding example for his successors: Nearly all of them would ever bow to the Lowland kings and do their bidding. Though the Campbell chiefs spoke Gaelic and adopted many of the traditions of the Highlands, their abiding role was to police the Gaels in their midst, as the loyal sheriffs of the Lowland kings.

Thus, whenever the king newly discovered some dominion over one of the clans, he could rely upon his Campbells. Rather than attempt to invade the Highlands, and risk costly defeats, he could expand his power rather cheaply; he needed only to employ a local clan to accomplish his deeds for him. As the king's authority grew further north and west, the authority of the Campbells grew with it. MacGregors, MacNaughtons, and so many others in the southern Highlands lost their homes, becoming feudal vassals of the king's most grateful friend. The Campbell territories expanded beyond Loch Awe and spread throughout the Lowlands, while Campbell lords sought favour in Edinburgh, obtaining lawyers' writs to seal courtly transactions.

For us, however, the king in Edinburgh was no master at all. How could we, ever, bow to a foreigner who wanted to make us his vassals? How could we, ever, bow to those who mocked us, who called us savages?

We fought with Robert the Bruce at Bannockburn, but we fought as his allies, not as his servants. The Lowlanders were free to adopt the English laws of barons and earls, but our people had been here, in these glens and upon these isles, long before feudal titles were even envisaged by those from the south.

No, we would keep to our path. We would stay to our ways, to the moulds that formed us. No matter how many ships the king commanded, no matter how many serfs he could force into battle, he knew the truth: The Kingdom of

Scotland, the kingdom he now claimed for himself, came about only because the Gaels had unified all Scots under a Highland sovereign.

We did not owe respect to him. He owed respect to *us*.

For the MacDonald chiefs were the leaders of the Gaels, the heirs to Somerled's country. They were called the Kings of the Hebrides by all, the Lords of the Isles, and throughout the 14th and 15th centuries, they controlled much more land than all the other Highland chiefs put together. Within Britain, only the kings of England and Scotland could claim more.

At Finlaggan, upon the island of Islay, the Lords of the Isles had their capital. There the Council of the Isles deliberated and resolved disputes. There Lord MacDonald granted charters and entertained guests in his Great Hall. A well-defended order prevailed throughout the lands of the Lordship, and poems and music attained new strengths. These were revered: The keener lines of the bards, a harp's muting strums, the pipes' breaking roar. Monks, too, praised and warned in pen strokes, and the artists rendered their filigree in gold.

Through courage, not courtiers' documents, the Lordship grew so widely that its branches nearly became clans of their own. Soon, besides the MacDonalds of Glen Coe, there were the MacDonalds of Glen Garry, of Clan Ranald, of Keppoch, and others.

Yet the Lowland kings of Scotland refused to accept that we should rule ourselves. They insisted that our land and our homes belonged to *them*, and so they pressed on into our country. With promises of power and money, they persuaded several other clans, not just the Campbells, to oppose us.

121

Our realm remained at its full strength, however, until 1475, when James III learned that John, Lord of the Isles, had allied himself with the Earl of Douglas, a Lowlander, to conquer Scotland and divide the country between the two of them. James used this alleged treason to full effect, rallying others to his cause, and John agreed to relinquish much of his territories upon the mainland of Scotland.

Still, our people chafed at John's meek submission; a leader who would bow, like that, is no leader at all. Many came out in support of John's son Angus, who rebelled against his father and campaigned to take back the lost lands. Now the Highlands and Isles erupted into a civil war. In 1484, or nearly then, Angus' forces met those of his father John at the Battle of Bloody Bay, off of the coast of the Isle of Mull. Angus was victorious, and took leadership of Clan Donald, but so many were killed on both sides, with much of the clan's fleet lying still beneath the waves.

Angus continued to lead the MacDonalds against the king, but we were weakened, hopelessly, by that war between father and son. After Angus was murdered in 1490, the new king, James IV, seized the title of Lord of the Isles. In 1493 and again in 1495, James sailed with his army to the Isles, where all of the Clan Donald chiefs paid homage to him.

All of the chiefs, that is, except for one: MacIain of Glen Coe.

Over the next several years, the king showed the other MacDonalds what rewards they would receive for their peaceable submission; he carved up Clan Donald lands and handed them over to his servants. Archibald Campbell, chief of his clan and recently minted Earl of Argyll, was appointed Royal Lieutenant over the lands that once had been the Lordship of the Isles. He received a lease of most of the Lordship's territories.

Only about fifteen years earlier, Archibald's sister had married Angus MacDonald, the victor at Bloody Bay, and she had given birth to a single boy, Donald, who had been recognised by all as the future Lord of the Isles. But Archibald's father, Colin Campbell, seeing what this baby could mean, had prevailed upon one of the king's close cousins to steal into Finlaggan, abduct the boy from his mother, and deliver him to Colin, his own grandfather.

Thus, when King James IV seized the Lordship of the Isles in 1493, he knew that the only heir to the Lordship was a boy, Donald, sitting in a prison at the Campbell stronghold of Innis Chonnel Castle. The master of that castle, Archibald, the Royal Lieutenant, soon turned his attention to the one clan that had refused to submit. In 1500, he went to his king and obtained a decree stating that the MacDonalds of Glen Coe should be evicted from our lands, and that Campbell should be free to people our home with anyone he wished.

My fathers learned of the decree, and, of course, decided this: They would walk deep into Campbell country on their own, attempt to break into a jail guarded by the Earl of Argyll's soldiers, and bring back Donald.

They gathered beside the River Coe, with the greater waters on the horizon. Their families did not weep. MacEanruig began piping. Now they followed MacIain south, toward Innis Chonnel, and I am certain that our bard told them:

When you pass beneath the last of the Three Sisters, think of the red stag upon the slope of *Coire Gabhail*. When you find high *Buachaille Etive Mòr* disappearing behind you, think of the ferns that remain under icy *Sgorr nam Fiannaidh*. The Campbell may throw you down, far from our burial isle, but your children will always know of this sun. Without daring, you are nothing.

It took a number of days before the events were known, and the initial reports were met with disbelief. But within a few days, many in the Highlands and the Isles had heard, and they said it to one another.

The MacDonalds of Glen Coe have rescued the Lord of the Isles. He is alive. Now he is protected, and the Islesmen are waiting for the word.

The rebellion has begun.

CHAPTER 15

DEAR MR. MACDONALD

Just two days after leaving Missouri, I was at my computer in New York, looking for my ancestors John McDonald and Elizabeth Downing, parents of my great-great-great-great-grandpa Hiram McDonald. But now there was this email from Mark MacDonald, the head of the Clan Donald DNA Project. Colin MacDonald was one of the three MacDonalds who matched Chuck, Grandma's brother, and Mark wrote this:

"Colin is from New Zealand, where he has been very active in Clan Donald affairs. Although he is not of paternal Somerled descent, he is currently proceeding before the Lord Lyon with either the tacit (or, I believe, the active) support of the remaining chiefs to be recognized as chief of the Glencoe branch. I have never personally reviewed his paperwork but I understand that he has excellent documentation of his descent from the youngest son of the chief in 1745."

The Lord Lyon Court of Arms is the authority under Scottish law for deciding who should be recognized as the chief of a clan, and it only took a moment to remember what

Bryan Sykes had said on the Isle of Skye. A chief had always been decided in exactly the same way a Y-chromosome is passed down—from father to son, and then from father to son, and then again from father to son.

Uncle Chuck had the DNA signature of the chiefs of the MacDonalds of Glencoe.

Just like the Clan Donald chiefs who sent in their cheek swabs to Sykes, Uncle Chuck and Colin had the same signature because they were both descended from a single, paternal line. I had to map this out, though, and within a few minutes, I found a Clan Donald site that had a Glencoe family tree on it, and I was able to match it up with what Mark's email said about Colin's line.

I began with Iain Fraoch, the first chief of the MacDonalds of Glencoe, and clicked on his son, also named Iain, and then clicked on *his* son Iain. And that took me to another clickable son Iain, and then another: There were eight Glencoe chiefs named Iain, from the 14th century into the late 16th. But now there was an Alasdair, and beginning with him, the clicks said this:

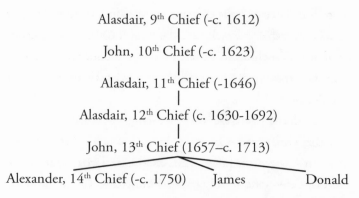

Alasdair, 9th Chief (-c. 1612)
|
John, 10th Chief (-c. 1623)
|
Alasdair, 11th Chief (-1646)
|
Alasdair, 12th Chief (c. 1630-1692)
|
John, 13th Chief (1657–c. 1713)

Alexander, 14th Chief (-c. 1750)   James   Donald

There was a footnote attached to Donald, the youngest brother of Alexander, and it read: "By tradition this line in males exists to the present day, possibly to Colin MacDonald of Canterbury, New Zealand." The chiefship had passed to Alexander and then to his son, but the chiefs' DNA signature had passed down to Donald, too, and to Donald's sons, and then to all of Donald's patrilineal descendants—even though none of them had ever been chief, and even though some of them emigrated to New Zealand.

And the same thing must have happened with my family. Uncle Chuck and Colin shared an ancestor, but in the generation after that shared ancestor, there'd been a split, with one brother leading down to my McDonald line and another brother leading down to Colin's line. The few DNA markers that Chuck and Colin *didn't* share were the signs of mutations that had occurred over the generations since that brotherly split.

Just when did the split happen? My ancestor John must have been born before 1790 or so, because his son Hiram was born in 1806, so John could have been the son or grandson or maybe even the great-grandson of Colin's ancestor Donald, who was born in the late 1690s or early 1700s. I didn't know anything about Donald's children or grandchildren, so for all I knew, Donald could have had descendants who ended up in Missouri.

But the DNA hinted at something else. Uncle Chuck matched Colin on 34 out of 37 markers, which meant that their most recent common ancestor—the father right above the brotherly split—was probably further back in the past.

They were a close match, but not *that* close. The three mismatched markers said that Chuck and Colin's most recent common ancestor was probably born in the 16th or 17th centuries, not the 18th.

I went back to that genealogy of the Glencoe chiefs from the Clan Donald site. Even if my John wasn't descended from Colin's ancestor Donald, he was probably descended from one of the chiefs who appeared above Donald. Was my John descended from the 13th chief, also named John? Or did my line break from the chiefly line earlier, with a younger brother of the 12th chief, or the 10th, or the 5th?

The DNA couldn't answer that question just yet, but I knew one thing already: If Chuck and Colin's signature was the signature of the Glencoe chiefs, then the official history was about to change.

According to that history, the first Glencoe chief, Iain Fraoch, was the son of Angus Og, the ally of Robert the Bruce at the Battle of Bannockburn. So, the story went, all the Glencoe chiefs from Iain Fraoch onward, all the MacIains, were patrilineal descendants of the MacDonald Lords of the Isles, and the MacDonald bards passed on this history, generation to new generation, until the books in English said it, too.

But Bryan Sykes had discovered that all of the living Clan Donald chiefs had the DNA signature of Somerled, the 12th century king who'd passed his lands and genes down to Angus Og, and I already knew that Chuck and Colin didn't have the Somerled signature. When Sykes wrote to those chiefs, he was writing to men whose families had held onto their lands and their titles for centuries. The last Glencoe chief, though, passed away long ago, and so there was no chance for Sykes to write to some titled MacIain gentleman and receive an eager cheek swab in the mail, and so Sykes never had to figure out just how to say:

It appears that there has been some sort of non-paternity event.

My ancestors weren't patrilineal descendants of Somerled, but they were treated as though they *had* been, every moment, every year. And so the real patriarch was hiding. His name was unknown, and his story had been left unsaid, or perhaps it had been quietly silenced because he was inconvenient to the clan. But his DNA was showing itself suddenly, and we knew his numbers.

Now I wanted to email Colin, or call him, or swim to New Zealand. His family records could say something about John McDonald, the father of my ancestor Hiram. I signed back into Chuck's personal page at the DNA company site and looked for Colin's email address, but the address listed was for Mark, the head of the Clan Donald DNA Project. Maybe Colin didn't use email, or he didn't want distant cousins to contact him.

According to Mark, the second match was Brundage MacDonald, the former High Commissioner for Clan Donald Canada. Brundage lived in Nova Scotia, and I knew that many Highlanders emigrated to Canada beginning in the late 18th century.

This brought a whole new possibility. Because of the distance between the U.S. and New Zealand, Colin and I probably didn't share an ancestor who lived in one and then emigrated to the other, so my line probably branched off from his back in Scotland. But Nova Scotia was just 50 miles or so from Maine. It was easy to envision a MacDonald coming to Pennsylvania, say, in the mid-1700s, and then one set of cousins found their way north and east, while another set of cousins went south and west.

Brundage's email address wasn't listed on Chuck's personal page, either, but Chuck's third match *did* have an email address listed, and I started typing. His name was Michael, but I went with "Mr. MacDonald," just to be safe. I introduced myself, wrote what I knew about my McDonald family, mentioned that Mark had revealed our shared descent from the Glencoe MacDonalds, and asked whether he might be willing to share what he knew about his MacDonald ancestors.

And within a few days, he wrote back. He didn't mention where he was from, and he didn't know a lot of details about his family history, but he was certain that his ancestors were from Glencoe, and he'd always been told that they were survivors of what happened in 1692. One of his relatives knew the family tree, so he'd reach out to her and then let me know what he found.

In the meantime, I was doing some online peeking.

Mark had said that Colin was an active member of Clan Donald New Zealand, so maybe I could just find out more by going to their site. I wasn't stalking, I told myself. No, I was just wondering whether Colin had willingly given out his phone number or email address, and that was very different from snooping. I hoped.

Soon I was reading what people had posted all around

the site—asking for clues about their MacDonald ancestors, saying hello to all their Clan Donald cousins out there. Then, suddenly, there was that name: Colin MacDonald.

His post was short, just a few lines long. In it, he mentioned that he was applying to be recognized as the chief of the MacDonalds of Glencoe. The post didn't say anything else about Colin, but it did give one final thing.

His email address.

I wrote to Mark, and he responded that it was perfectly fine to email Colin. And as it turned out, Brundage had given Mark his email address a few years before.

All right then, let's start with Colin. Let's start with "Dear Mr. MacDonald." I said hello, laid out what I knew about my McDonalds of Missouri, and mentioned that Mark had told me about Colin's descent from the Glencoe chiefs. I included a link to the Clan Donald site I'd found, the one with the footnote that referenced him by name. "It would be wonderful if you'd be willing to share more details," I wrote.

The next day, sitting at my computer, I looked at my inbox and saw the name Colin MacDonald in bold. "Dear Ryan," he wrote, "How nice to hear from you."

Yes, he'd been working for a year and a half on his application to be recognized as the chief of the MacDonalds of Glencoe, and he'd seen the Clan Donald site's reference to him, and he was receiving wonderful support from Mac-Donald folks worldwide. Still, the Lord Lyon Court of Arms in Edinburgh required airtight proof, and though Colin was clearly descended from the chiefs, he only had the required documentation back to the year 1788. So a genealogist in

Scotland was working to uncover the pre-1788 records. Colin's great-great-grandfather Donald, great-grandson of the Donald I'd found online, emigrated from Scotland to New Zealand in 1840, and the family had been there since.

He finished his email by writing, "I have been to Scotland three times and always feel like I am going home."

I wondered what he looked like, and sounded like. I wondered what it would be like to know, your whole life, that you were descended from the chiefs of this glen. I wondered about his family. How many cousins did I have, out there, on the other side of the earth, where summer is winter and they grow up playing rugby? One thing, though, I knew from Colin's email—my line must have branched off from his in Scotland, as I'd suspected before.

Now, on to my Canadian cousin Brundage. I began, again, with "Dear Mr. MacDonald," and let him know who I was, and recounted what I knew about my McDonald ancestors, and asked if he'd be willing to share notes.

Two days later, before the coffee had even begun brewing, I saw: "Good Morning Mr. Littrell." Brundage apologized for such a dreadfully tardy response, and wrote that he was descended from a man named Angus MacDonald, of Glencoe, whose three sons emigrated to Nova Scotia in the early 1800s. "Anything I can do to help you in your research will no doubt help us both," he wrote, and he offered to send me his MacDonald family tree. He closed with the words *Beannachd leat*. Goodbye.

And a few days later, after I'd emailed him back with my thanks and with more tidbits about our newfound DNA cousins, Brundage sent me his family tree. At the top was Angus MacDonald, who was born in Glencoe in about 1730 and died in Glencoe at some unknown date. His wife was Janet McIntyre, and her birth date and her death date were unknown, but it was known that she had drowned, and it was remembered that people had always called her "the strong woman who was good to the poor."

I went through the list of Angus and Janet's children and grandchildren, because maybe one of them was my ancestor John McDonald. I saw that Angus and Janet had one son named John, but Brundage's research showed that this John lived his whole adult life with his wife Mary Stuart and their children in Nova Scotia, from 1807 onwards, so it was un-likely that he could have been the same man as my ancestor John, who'd married Elizabeth Downing by the early 1800s and whose children were soon in Missouri. And Angus and Janet had two grandchildren named John, but both were born way too late to have been my ancestor John.

So the DNA couldn't reveal just where, in the past, my line had split off from Colin's or Brundage's, at least not yet. But the DNA results made clear that my John McDonald, if he were going to be discovered at all, would only be dis-covered through documents—through census entries or tax charges or scrawled wills.

Now, I'd already found the family tree on Ancestry.com that said Cyrus McDonald, my ancestor Hiram's probable brother, had gotten married in Warren County, Kentucky. That gave me a place to begin.

I went to the online Warren County censuses for 1810

and 1820, and sure enough, there was a John McDonald. In both censuses, his age, his wife's age, and the ages and genders of their children were consistent with what I knew about my McDonalds. And there was no John McDonald in the 1830 Warren County census, which jibed with my Elizabeth's appearance as the head of her own household in Missouri that year.

Then again, here was an Elizabeth McDonald in Warren County in 1820, and her family looked very much like the John McDonald family, with their ages and genders. This Elizabeth could have been my Elizabeth, too, because my John might have died or left the family before 1820, in which case the 1820 John McDonald would have been another man completely. I couldn't prove that the 1810 John McDonald was my John, either, because I couldn't rule out the chance that this John just happened to share a name with my John, along with some convenient dates.

Still, these 1810 and 1820 Warren County census entries hinted at some things. There were two Angus McDonalds here—an older man in 1810 and a younger one in 1820. Angus was a very Highland name, and my new cousin Brundage's ancestor was called Angus, so this might have been a family name. And John lived just two farms away from an Allen McDonald in 1820, so maybe they were related.

I searched Ancestry.com again, and then searched everywhere else online, but Warren County, Kentucky wasn't telling me any more. There were no McDonalds or McDaniels in the 1800 census, the first one for the county, and no online marriage record for my John and my Elizabeth, and no tax records, no deeds and no baptisms and no burials, no transcribed remembrances.

It took just a moment to find out that there are daily, non-stop flights from New York to Nashville, and you can rent a car and head north, take I-65, mostly, and you can be at the Warren County, Kentucky courthouse within two hours of landing. Ask to look at the records, bring your laptop along, bring your notes along, and hope the hotel has a decent burger.

But then I got a new email from Harriett.

Harriett Worrell and I had been exchanging emails since her response to my recent post on Ancestry.com, where I'd let the world know that my ancestor Hiram seemed to be related to those McDonalds who lived in Lincoln County, Missouri and Pike County, Missouri beginning in 1830. Harriett was active in the Pike County Genealogical Society, and was doing research for a descendant of Cyrus, my Hiram's probable brother. I'd mentioned to her that Cyrus might have gotten married in Warren County, Kentucky before the family's migration to Missouri.

In this new email, Harriett told me she'd followed up on my clue, and had found a genealogist in Warren County who was searching in the county courthouse for Cyrus and his parents. Perhaps there wouldn't be any genealogical road trip for me, after all.

And, she said, he was already making discoveries. She sketched them in a few, fast sentences, and I thought I understood what she was getting at. But I needed to see the picture, the context, in order for things to make sense. I wanted to walk the cul-de-sacs. Would she mind maybe mailing a copy of the findings?

She wouldn't mind at all, she said, and a few days later, I opened my mailbox to find an envelope full of papers. The genealogist, Bill Danlon, had written his report as a chronicle, taking Harriett—and now me—through his digging, from beginning to end. Reading down the lists, reading through his notes, nearly put me in his shoes.

Bill started off by looking at the microfilm copies of the Warren County tax lists from 1797 to 1823. The federal census takers only came around once a decade, but the Kentucky tax man made sure to stop by once a year, so looking at the tax lists meant Bill could track the McDonalds of Warren County from one year to the next.

There were no McDonalds or McDaniels in the county from 1797 to 1808, but in 1809, Angus made his first appearance. The 1810 list was missing, but in 1811, there were John and Angus. And in 1812, there were John, Angus, and Allen. So it went for the next several years, with John and Angus and Allen all paying taxes, but Angus disappeared after 1819. There *was* an Angus in 1820, but based upon the value of his estate, this was almost certainly the younger Angus I'd found in the census records. Soon, then, Elizabeth appeared in the tax lists, and the location of her land, and the value of her estate, suggested that she was the older Angus' widow—and the Elizabeth I'd found living in the county in 1820.

So, Bill wondered, who might have been our Cyrus' father, just based on this first set of records? The older Angus was a candidate, because he had three young, unnamed sons in the 1810 census, and Cyrus was born in about 1808. But John was a candidate, too; he had three young sons in 1810, and in 1820 had three sons between 10 and 16. Candidate number three was Allen, who didn't appear in 1810, but in 1820 had one son in that 10 to 16 bracket.

Then Bill turned to the marriage records and found the September 22, 1828 marriage bond for Cyrus McDaniel and Elizabeth Lemastes. This had to be our Cyrus, because I knew from the Missouri records that the name of our Cyrus' wife was Elizabeth Lemasters. That family tree on Ancestry.com, the one connecting Cyrus to Warren County, had been right all along.

A marriage bond was the groom's promise to the court that nothing prohibited the couple from getting married, but in this case there was something more. Because Cyrus was under the age of twenty-one, he didn't just have to sign a bond—he also had to obtain his father's consent. That's why another sentence was added to the back of the marriage bond: "I do certify that I am willing a marriage license may issue for my son Syrus McDaniel and Elizabeth Lemastes."

Underneath was an X, next to the name of Elizabeth McDonald. Cyrus' father must have passed away, and Cyrus' mother Elizabeth had given the parental consent instead.

Now, Bill asked: Was there a male McDonald in Warren County who died before September 22, 1828, and had been married to an Elizabeth? From online family trees and message postings, I knew that candidate number three for the role of Cyrus' father, Allen McDonald, lived well past 1828, and that his wife wasn't named Elizabeth, so he couldn't be the one.

Bill began looking at records of land deeds, because these often listed the wife of the man who was buying or selling land. And deed after deed showed only one Elizabeth married to a male McDonald, and his name was Angus. Candidate number two. Was this Cyrus' father?

Bill turned to the wills and court records, since it appeared that Angus, husband of Elizabeth, had passed away in the county, and sure enough, here were several court entries in 1819 and 1820 about the deceased Angus' estate. His wife Elizabeth was appointed to administer the estate, and in this one entry from October 3, 1820, Elizabeth was legally recognized as the guardian of all of her and Angus' children under the age of twenty-one. Their names were Fanny, William, Charles, Sarah, John, Henry and Polly.

No Cyrus. No Hiram. No Darius, no James or Rebecca, no Thomas or Betsy or Patsy, no Ezekiel Downing McDonald. Angus and Elizabeth *couldn't* be the parents of my McDonalds, the young adults who appeared in Missouri with my Elizabeth beginning in the 1830s.

Bill continued looking through the wills, and then the court records, and it was only there that he discovered that one other McDonald had died in the 1820s. His name was John. And at the county court on May 5, 1828, the right to administer John's estate was granted to his wife.

Her name? Elizabeth.

John and Elizabeth had to be Cyrus' parents, and this was the same Cyrus McDonald who lived in Lincoln County and Pike County, Missouri from 1830 onwards. So the Elizabeth who lived in Warren County, Kentucky, and who was the widow of John, had to be the same woman as the Elizabeth who was buried in Lincoln County, Missouri, and whose gravestone read "Consort of John." And my Missouri trip had shown that *this* Elizabeth, the Elizabeth who was buried out behind my cousin Judy's house, was the mother of my Hiram.

Now I knew it for certain: My great-great-great-great-grandfather Hiram McDonald's parents were the John and Elizabeth McDonald who lived in Warren County, Kentucky.

This is why Elizabeth left. This is why she left her life in Kentucky behind. She had to find a new home for herself and her twelve children because her husband had passed away. Even her young, married son Cyrus came along to Missouri.

But what about John? How did he die? There were no obituaries back then, and Bill hadn't looked for a will or a burial record for John, so I didn't know much about him. Still, I wondered whether Bill's discoveries might say something about John's family, his siblings or cousins or parents.

I went back to the start of Bill's chronicle, looking for clues to John's relatives. And here, right at the beginning, was something I'd barely noticed before. The tax lists of 1809 to 1823 showed that Allen, Angus, and my ancestor John didn't just live in the same county; they lived close to one another. Again and again, they were listed together, not because they shared a surname but because they lived nearly together, by Little Beaver Dam Creek, by Indian Creek and Alexander Creek, even out in the grasslands known as The Barrens.

Then, reading Bill's list of marriage records, I saw that the young Angus McDonald who first appeared as a head of household in the 1820 census was the son of Allen, who had to give his consent in order for young Angus to be married in 1819. Angus seemed to be a family name—in Allen's family. That wasn't all: When Allen's daughter Patsy was married in 1822, my ancestor John served as the witness.

So were John, Allen, and the older Angus brothers? And if they *were* brothers, who were their parents?

CHAPTER 16

AN LINN
NAN CREACH

Cha robh an rìgh ro dhèidheil air ar neart, a-rèir coltais.

The king, it would seem, did not take kindly to our strength.

He was dismayed to learn that the MacDonalds of Glen Coe had just now plucked our young Lord of the Isles from the cage of his most able servant Archibald Campbell, the Earl of Argyll, the Royal Lieutenant. He surely was dismayed to learn, once and again throughout the years 1501 and 1502, that clan upon clan had pledged support for our Donald: The MacLeods of the Isle of Lewis, the Camerons of Loch Eil, the MacLeans and the MacKinnons, the MacNeills of the Isle of Barra, and so many others.

For all that, the MacDonalds were unable to summon quite the force we once could. The Battle of Bloody Bay, when Donald's grandfather fought his father upon the sea, had sapped us, with much of our navy wrecked. Thus, as soon as the king's dismay turned to resolve, he called upon his willing servants and chose to exhibit his might by sending his ships north and west. The chiefs of the clans knew that this was not the time to risk all.

Yet, even with the king's demonstration, we had won everything that we needed. For while he might claim dominion over the Highlands and the Isles, we continued to govern ourselves just as we wished. A chief was still the king over his own lands. Perhaps we could not overcome the crown in Edinburgh, but our rebellion proved that it could not overcome us, either. It could neither subdue us, nor police us, nor force the ways of the south upon us. For the rest of the 16th century, and quite into the 17th, an unsaid truce lurked behind nearly every Highland revolt, just as it lurked in the sighs accompanying each seeming reconciliation: We would make a convenient show of pledging loyalty to the kings of Scotland from time to time, and those kings would, for the greater part, leave us to ourselves.

So it was that my ancestors remained here in the glen, beneath the peaks of the *Feinn*. My fathers had proven to the Campbell that our *dùthchas* could be severed from us only with our heads.

So it was that the bards at Achtriachtan still praised Mac-Iain, and still had poems to tell of his undaunted heart. They still spoke of the wine cups and panelled walls of his house at Polveig. The children still learned the old names for every stream, for each hollow and hillock. The heather by the River Coe had no regard for the fall of the Lordship of the Isles, and the fattening cattle during the spring cared little about a royal court, away in the Lowlands. Our shielings upon the Black Mount still gave us shelter for the summer, and autumn brought the festival of *Samhuinn*, as ever before.

Without one monarch to unite all of the Gaels, however, we could rely no longer upon the greater Clan Donald to govern our neighbours. No longer would fear of the Lord of the Isles suffice to shield us. Like the MacDonalds of Keppoch, of the Clan Ranald, of Glen Garry and of elsewhere, we became fully a clan of our own, maintaining our bonds to those kinsmen but cultivating our sovereignty, as well, safeguarding the glen upon our terms. MacIain, the people would say, is the arching tree that gives us shelter.

We were quickly accustomed to this new age, this time of forays, only because we already had the heart for it. The *togail creach*, the cattle raid, had for centuries been a test and show of our valour, just as it had been for our neighbours who longed for the bounty of Glen Coe. To walk away from my lands knowing that I may fall, forever, and yet to return with the riches of cattle: All of this augured courage on the battlefield. So, too, did a sudden defence, protecting my children's milk and meat when raiders made their way, somehow, into the glen. Indeed, MacIain's son only could become chief once he had proven himself in an expedition, leading the other young ones who had yet to show themselves. None of it was robbery, of course, for the man whose cattle had been taken yesterday was expected to take mine today, if he could but bring courage enough. If he could not, it was no fault of mine, and thus the bulls and cows had come to the proper place.

These forays were only the wee signals of a greater struggle, throughout the Highlands and the Isles. Everywhere in Somerled's old kingdom, clan turned upon clan, with hopes of controlling much more than cattle. Under the MacDonalds, we Gaels had been no more warlike than any other people, but the same forces that gave an independence to the people of Glen Coe also promised sovereignty for all of the other clans: As the king was not strong enough to replace those he had unseated, every clan was newly emboldened to battle, to settle old disputes by the sword.

The monarchs of the Lowlands endeavoured to show their rule, still, by picking sides in those clan feuds, by rewarding grateful followers with titles, or by executing those rebels they could ensnare. In this, they relied upon their steadfast friends, who loyally knew of Highland politics, who loyally knew how best to manage the Gaels. From son to son, Campbells were elevated, and their holdings grew. Their young men were quickly married to noblewomen from the south, thus strengthening valuable alliances with the Lowland lords. Their daughters were quickly married to the sons of Highland chiefs, in the hope that some occasional favour might be obtained.

Whether it was a cattle raid or a clan battle that reached their ears, the king and his servants persisted in regarding Highland people as the most incorrigible barbarians, what with our unaltered superstitions, our thirst for blood, our primitive language. Upon a number of occasions, they provided us with a civilising example, as when the Earl of Lennox laid waste to MacDonald lands, and when the heads of our Donald's supporters were placed just above the town gates at Elgin, and when the Earl of Huntly's followers stabbed the Earl of Moray in a cave. These lessons were regrettably intermittent through much of the 16th century.

We were, thus, so very gratified when King James VI of Scotland, near the close of the century, at last deigned to bless us with his justice in full. To begin, he took away the lands of the MacLeods of Lewis, awarded them to Lowlanders, and arranged for the colonisation of that isle, just as he would later do across the Irish Sea in Ulster. The aim, stated forthrightly, was "to plant Lowlandmen in the Isles and transport the inhabitants to the mainland, where they might learn civility." The colonists were given liberty to use "slaughter, mutilation, fire-raising or other inconveniences" as necessary for "rooting out the barbarous inhabitants."

In the southern Highlands, James expunged the name of MacGregor, forcing the MacGregors into the choice between renouncing their family or being hanged, and then ordered the Campbell chief "to lay mercy aside, and by justice and the sword to root out and extirpate all of that race." James occasionally showed his hospitality, as well. He once invited three chiefs to Edinburgh so that they could consult with him and his Privy Council concerning the governance of the Isles, and the Council promised the chiefs safe passage. When they arrived, he imprisoned them, only allowing them to go free once they had paid him a large sum and had pledged obedience to him and his cousin, Queen Elizabeth of England.

Yet James' most helpful contribution to our eventual justice came from his laws. Passed through the Parliament of Scotland in 1609, and hardened in the succeeding years, the king's statutes forced our chiefs to send their eldest children to school in the Lowlands, where the children had to remain until they had learned to read and write in English. Parish schools were set up in the Highlands, teaching in English alone. Our bards were outlawed. Ordinary clansmen were forbidden from carrying any weapon, and limits were placed upon our drinking of wine and whisky.

Through much of the Gaelic country, where the king's power did not fully reach, these laws were, lamentably, unable to deliver us wholly to advancement. Some of the chiefs sent their heirs to Lowland schools, but our ancestors' tongue was still ours, and many of our well-born sons studied at the University of Paris besides. The bards still recited our people's histories beside the fire. Great and common men still held to our defence, and it was said that many a chief was yet in the habit of attending a feast accompanied by two servants with a wheelbarrow, who stood behind him for hours and then carted him home at the close of the evening.

Behind James' boldness was his new station, his new power. Just a few years before, in 1603, this Lowlander of Scotland had become the King of England, and not through strength in battle, but through dynastic luck; his dear cousin Elizabeth, the only surviving grandchild of the English King Henry VII, had died childless, and as he was the great-great-grandson of Henry VII on both his father and mother's side, James had been next in line to the throne of the English.

He had quickly left for the south, and had been received warmly by his subjects. He had promised to return to Scotland every few years, but came back only once during the twenty-two years he reigned in London. His son, the future King Charles I, grew up as an Englishman. The laws passed by his Parliament in Edinburgh, the civilising ones, might well have had this as preface: I now have the English navy behind me, and the English army.

Alasdair, the eleventh chief of the MacDonalds of Glen Coe, observing events from far away, saw by 1638 that such undivided support would never be enjoyed by the new King Charles. Although Charles was a Protestant, the Puritans in England and the Presbyterians in the Lowlands of Scotland suspected him of being not Protestant enough, with secret designs to return both countries to Catholicism. For more than a decade, as well, they and their allies in the Parliaments of both England and Scotland had quarrelled with Charles over the limits of royal authority. Civil war broke out in Scotland in 1639, and in England three years later.

Like all MacDonalds and most Highlanders, Alasdair of Glen Coe and his people entered the war on the side of Charles, but our support naturally did not spring from any loyalty to this son of James VI. No, we took this side because Archibald Campbell, Earl of Argyll, and the whole of his followers had taken precisely the opposite side.

The Campbell reach had so expanded that Archibald was the most powerful man in Scotland, beside Charles, and his betrayal of his king delivered us an opportunity. At last, after a century and a half, the MacDonalds might again be acknowledged as the lords of the Gaels. Campbell might be returned properly to his compliant, southern hills. Once more, Somerled's grandsons might rule over our lands.

Our first chance arrived at the 2nd of February, 1645, when we, outnumbered, met the Campbells beside Inverlochy Castle. The men of Glen Coe were at the front of the line, next to our Irish and Highland cousins, as the Campbells and their few Highland allies lined up across us, flanked by Lowland infantry. After firing a single volley, the Irish charged, and the Lowlanders panicked and fled. Campbell's Highland men stood their ground longer, of course, but even they could not withstand the charge of Clan Donald.

The Earl of Argyll himself watched from his galley in the loch while his army was utterly ruined. Throughout the Highlands and the Isles, his downfall was celebrated in the bards' poetry and songs.

In England, however, King Charles was being routed by the forces of Parliament. Even in Scotland, with their armies replenished, the Lowlanders won a victory against the king at Philiphaugh, and in May of 1646, Charles was taken prisoner. On the 2nd of June, our commander, Lord Montrose, received a letter from Charles, ordering him to disband our army.

For us, in the glen, that would not happen quite so quickly. Two days after Lord Montrose received Charles' letter, the MacDonalds of Glen Coe learned that the daughter of Robert Campbell of Glen Orchy, cousin to the Earl of Argyll, was to be married soon at Finlarig by Loch Tay, so that all of the gentry of Glen Orchy would be away at the wedding celebrations. For the better of two years, the Campbells had plundered MacDonald lands, and now there was a chance of revenge. Our chief Alasdair, along with Angus MacDonald of Achnancoichean, son of the chief of Keppoch, led the men of Glen Coe and Keppoch into the Campbells' lands and made off with a large spoil of cattle.

When the Campbells heard of this, they rushed from Finlarig and caught up with the MacDonalds, who drew our swords. Big Archibald MacPhail of Glen Coe, just before he charged, took the time to pray: Lord, if you cannot join the MacDonalds at this time, please do not join the Campbells, either.

Perhaps Big Archibald's prayer had been answered, it later was said, for the MacDonalds decimated those Campbells with fury, slaying nearly all of their leading men. Though Alasdair of Glen Coe and Angus of Achnancoichean fell, the sons of Iain Fraoch had once again proven our fortitude.

The Campbells' great leader, for his part, did not forget that his sole compass was his own self-interest. Archibald Campbell, Earl of Argyll, swiftly allied himself with Oliver Cromwell, the commander of the English Parliament's army. Then Campbell established a Scottish government that was wholly friendly to Cromwell. Yet when Cromwell and his supporters executed King Charles in early 1649, Scots were revolted, even the king's opponents. Campbell felt about for the winds and promptly turned into a Royalist, joining with other members of the Scottish Parliament in recognising Charles' son, Charles II, as king.

The MacDonalds lamented: We only entered into this Anglo-Saxon feud in order to daunt the Campbell, but he has come around to our side.

While they waited for Charles II to return to Scotland, the English turned their eyes upon Ireland. Like Highlanders, the native Irish were no admirers of the English Crown, but had supported the king when compelled to choose sides.

Cromwell and his massive army landed at Dublin in August of 1649, and the Irish fought with such valour, but the numbers of the English, their cannons and naval blockades, were too much. One town wall after another fell. The English murdered thousands of women and children, besides soldiers and old men. They burned crops and churches. Famines spread. Most of the native landowners had their lands taken from them, and many of the Irish people were sold into slavery, to work on English plantations in the New World.

It was at this time that the son of our fallen chief Alasdair finally returned to our glen. He was named Alasdair, as well.

A young man, barely older than twenty, he had been studying at Paris throughout the recent troubles, and all of the people of Glen Coe rejoiced when he appeared. He was six feet, seven inches tall, with broad shoulders, and with hair hanging long, nearly to his heart. All saw that he was clever, that he could be brave, and it was thought that he was fair.

Like his fathers before him, Alasdair stood atop a pyramid of stones and was recognised as our chief, the twelfth MacIain. All around him gathered our people, while one of our bards recited Alasdair's descent from Iain Fraoch, from Somerled and Conn of the Hundred Battles. The bard told Alasdair of the courage of the ancestors, and reminded him of their generosity. That evening, as the whisky overtook just a few, as several of the younger ones danced about the fires, perhaps some remarked that the sun had shone with uncommon brightness upon *Beinn Fhada* today, and that the tide at the loch had seemed uncommonly gentle.

He was so very young then.

CHAPTER 17

ON THESE
STONES

The online article in *Scots Heritage Magazine* had been written recently, and it began: "Alistair MacDonald is not a rich man; far from it. Like his father and grandfather before him, he has been a crofter in Glencoe since he was a boy."

A few years back, the article recounted, Alistair was nearing retirement when he learned that 130 acres in Glencoe had come up for sale. The chiefs of the MacDonalds of Glencoe and their cousins had sold off the clan's lands, piecemeal, beginning in the early 19th century. Then the lands had been divided, resold, and divided again and resold again, until these 130 acres were all that remained in any single owner's hands. That single owner, it turned out, had once employed Alistair as a shepherd.

Alistair and his wife Rosalin wanted to buy the land, and they knew that the Scottish Government might be willing to step in and help—it was common in the Highlands for local people to band together, garner public financing, and buy large tracts from willing landowners. But Alistair and Rosalin refused public funds.

"If I accepted State money," Alistair said, "conservationists from Edinburgh or Glasgow would soon be telling us how to run the place and I don't agree at all with their theories of land management. All they want to do is lock up the land and forget about the communities that live here."

So Alistair and Rosalin came up with the money on their own. They went to their family, and to their friends, and they borrowed. When they presented their offer to the executors of the estate of Lord Strathcona, they knew that the other bidders had offered much more money.

But Lord Strathcona's executors chose Alistair and Rosalin. They chose this idea of a Glencoe Heritage Trust, which would belong only to the local people. Alistair and Rosalin wouldn't own the land, but the debt would be all theirs. The purchase included a one-half share of the burial isle, out in Loch Leven.

"You cannot put a price on history," Alistair said. "Glencoe means more to the MacDonalds than mere money. This is the land of our forefathers. Our history is written in blood on these stones. To us this is a sacred site. It's where we are who we are."

The article said that Alistair's father and grandfather had lived in Glencoe, and so I wondered: What if his great-grandfather had lived there, too, and his great-great-grandfather, and his ancestors? What if Alistair were my cousin?

I wanted to contact him and ask about his family's history, but I didn't even make it to "Dear Mr. MacDonald." Because I could already hear how my email would sound: Hello, I'm an American who found this story about you at

ScotsHeritageMagazine.com, and I've never even been to Glencoe, but I think what you did was great, and how about a DNA sample?

All I could say, anyway, was that I was descended from a John McDonald who died in Warren County, Kentucky, U.S.A. in 1828. John very well could have been born in America, the son or grandson or great-grandson of immigrants, in which case Alistair probably wouldn't have any records mentioning him. It was better to put off emailing Alistair until I'd uncovered my immigrant McDonald, or at least tried. Besides, it's one thing to contact someone whom you know is a DNA match. It's another thing to go trawling.

But then, on a Friday afternoon, a match came to *me*.

The email was from the DNA company, and it took me to Uncle Chuck's personal page. There I saw a new name: Lachlan Buchanan MacDonald. He was Chuck's closest match; they shared 35 out of 37 DNA markers. Lachlan had given his email address, so I started writing, introducing myself and admitting that I hadn't yet uncovered my ancestor John McDonald's parents. Still, I told him, all three of our shared DNA matches knew that their MacDonalds came from one particular place. "Do you know whether your MacDonald ancestors were from Glencoe?" I asked.

Just a few hours later, a message arrived from Diane Mac-Donald. "Hello Cousin Ryan," she wrote. "My husband Lachie is a Luddite and doesn't use a 'pooter,' so I'm his secretary." Yes, Lachie's patrilineal ancestors were from Glencoe—they fled the glen sometime after 1692.

And Lachie and Diane were Scots.

They lived near Glasgow, where Diane was an administrator with the National Health Service and Lachie was a dentist. Diane didn't mention where she was born and raised, but she wrote that Lachie was from Lismore, an island off the west coast of Scotland, and he was a native Gaelic speaker.

"We have long memories for the 13th February, 1692 and all that!" she wrote. "You have dozens of rellies, I'm afraid... perhaps you will visit us sometime." She promised to send me Lachie's family tree, and closed with the words *Slainte Mhath*. Good health.

I searched for Lachie's home isle of Lismore on the map, and saw that it lay only fifteen miles or so from Glencoe, just one hundred yards off the mainland at one point. The ancestors of Uncle Chuck's closest DNA match didn't just remain in Scotland; they remained in the Highlands, and never stopped speaking Gaelic.

If I were more closely related to Lachie than to Uncle Chuck's other matches, then Lachie's ancestors who fled from Glencoe might have been *my* ancestors, too. Did my MacDonald line branch off from Lachie's line after 1692, with one brother remaining in the Highlands and the other leaving for America?

In order to answer that question, I'd first have to uncover my immigrant ancestor, and that meant returning to the mystery of my ancestor John McDonald of Warren County, Kentucky.

Bill Danlon, the genealogist in Warren County, had discovered the 1828 records about my John's estate, along with all those clues linking John to Allen and Angus McDonald.

From Bill, I suspected that John was the brother of Allen and Angus.

Still, Bill hadn't finished looking at the county's records. What if there were still some piece of paper at the courthouse in Bowling Green revealing my John's parents, or at least saying *something* about his family?

So I emailed Bill and asked if he'd be willing to look some more. Sure, he replied, he'd be happy to.

He did his searching in a few stages, but each time he had the same truth to report: He'd been unable to find anything in Warren County that shed light on my John's origins. John and Angus were ordered by the court to view a proposed road in 1816, and John bought some goods from Angus' estate in 1819, but there was nothing else linking John to any other McDonalds. John didn't leave a will, and the records detailing the administration of his estate had been lost. Bill had looked at everything, he assured me. The records just weren't there.

But at the same time I was emailing back and forth with Bill, thanking him and waiting for results, I was coming onto another path. Maybe no one would ever find a document saying who my John's parents were, but I had reason to believe that John was the brother of Allen and Angus. What if *their* parents were known?

Google took me to the McDonald forum at Genealogy. com, where I typed in "Allen." There I found a post, and then another, and then another, all saying the same thing: Allen and Angus McDonald of Warren County, Kentucky really were brothers, and their father was a man named Angus McDonald, Sr. This Angus McDonald, Sr. left a will in Garrard

County, Kentucky in 1826, naming his wife Nancy and his daughters Elizabeth, Nancy, Patsy, Polly, Peggy and Sally.

The names of his three sons? Allen, Angus, Jr., and John.

This just *had* to be my ancestor John.

Still, the 1826 will didn't mean a thing unless I could be certain that the people posting at Genealogy.com were right. How could I know for sure that Angus McDonald, Sr. of Garrard County was the father of Allen and Angus McDonald of Warren County, the probable brothers of my ancestor John?

I started by looking through the census records at Ancestry.com. In 1810, there were only three Allen McDonalds in the entire United States who fit the age profile of our Allen—the one who lived near my ancestor John—and one of those three Allens just happened to be in Garrard County, Kentucky, the same county where Angus McDonald, Sr. lived. From Bill's research, I knew that our Allen didn't appear near my ancestor John in Warren County until 1812, which suggested that he was identical to this Allen McDonald who was in Garrard County in 1810.

Now I looked at the 1820 census, and sure enough, there was no Allen McDonald in Garrard County that year, when our Allen was recorded in Warren County. The facts hinted at a story: Our Allen lived near his father Angus McDonald, Sr. in Garrard County in 1810, but soon moved away to live near his two brothers Angus Jr. and John in Warren County.

Then I got an email from Jim McDonald, a patrilineal descendant of Allen who'd posted at Genealogy.com. Jim revealed that Angus McDonald, Sr.'s 1826 will didn't just list the names of his three sons; it also said that Angus, Jr. had passed away, while Allen and John were still alive. I knew that Angus McDonald of Warren County—the one who lived near Allen and my ancestor John—died before 1826, and so he was almost certainly the same man as this Angus, Jr., the deceased son named in Angus McDonald, Sr.'s will.

The online posters were right: Allen and Angus McDonald of Warren County really were the sons of Angus McDonald, Sr. of Garrard County.

Still, even though the records showed that my ancestor John probably was the son of Angus McDonald, Sr., I couldn't eliminate the possibility that my John was an unrelated McDonald who just happened to live near Angus McDonald, Sr.'s two sons. But if a patrilineal descendant of Allen or Angus, Jr. closely matched Uncle Chuck's DNA signature, then I'd have no doubts.

I'd get to go trawling for DNA, after all.

I emailed back Jim McDonald and asked if he'd be willing to do the cheek swab. Jim was from Arkansas, but had lived in Houston for more than thirty years, and had been researching the McDonalds for a while. Yes, he told me, he'd submit his DNA.

And it was about two months later that I got the email from the DNA company. Jim was a perfect match with Uncle Chuck, the only perfect match out of tens of thousands of DNA samples. Every DNA marker in Jim's signature matched Chuck's. No one in the U.S. even came close to matching the two of them.

My great-great-great-great-great-great-grandfather was the man named Angus McDonald, who left his will in Gar-

157

rard County, Kentucky in 1826.

From the later census records, I could tell that he passed away before 1830, and that Nancy, his wife at the time of his death, was born in the 1770s—which meant she was too young to be my John's mother. So my McDonald family tree now looked like this:

Angus McDonald (-bet. 1826 and 1830)
|
John McDonald (-1828), m. Elizabeth Downing
|
Hiram McDonald (1806-1882), m. Nancy Buchanan
|
William Duncan McDonald (1855-1935), m. Georgianna Wilson
|
Will McDonald (1875-1964), m. Linnie Hagan
|
Lee McDonald (my great-grandpa), m. Mary Bridgewater
|
Betty McDonald (my grandma), m. Don McCord

Another of the online posters, Leroy McDonald, knew that my ancestor John's brother Allen was born on December 6, 1774, and Allen probably wasn't even the youngest of his siblings. So Allen's father, my ancestor Angus, was probably born before 1750, and almost certainly before 1755. Relatively few Scottish Highlanders emigrated to America before the late 1740s, but from then until the beginning of the Revolutionary War in 1775, thousands of them left, often headed for Maryland, North Carolina, or Virginia.

Was Angus my immigrant ancestor?

Now I was ready to contact Alistair MacDonald of Glencoe, who might be able to tell me more. My Canadian cousin Brundage had mentioned that he knew Alistair, and in my email, I let slip my DNA connection to Brundage. I asked Alistair whether he might have any suggestions about uncovering my ancestor Angus' parents. Then I looked over my email, made sure I didn't sound like a crazed fan, and clicked "Send."

A few days later, there was a response from Alistair: "You appear to have got back some way in your genealogy. We have the family tree which Brundage sent to us some time ago, do you have the same?" He said that my ancestor Angus' father—if we just knew his name—might have fought in the rebellion of 1745. He said that his and Rosalin's son Alexander had transcribed all the gravestone inscriptions on the burial isle, and that he had some lists of passengers on ships leaving Scotland after 1745.

"If this is of any help, please let us know," he finished.

It's a big help, and much appreciated, I wrote back. I told him about the Clan Donald DNA Project and the few things I knew about my Angus, and he responded by letting me know of the records that existed in the glen before 1800.

As I emailed him back, I didn't want to seem like I was inviting myself over. But Penny and I had already booked our flights, and we were almost done packing, and we'd made plans to meet up with my new cousin Lachie and his wife Diane. So, in my email, I just told Alistair that if he wanted to contact me for any reason, he could find me at the Clachaig Inn, in Glencoe.

CHAPTER 18

DUINE UASAL

Bha beartas Alasdair MhicDhòmhnaill ' na shùilean.

The wealth of Alasdair MacDonald was in his eyes.

He saw the green lying about the wild flowers, and the salted venison above our fires, the salmon carried up from the waters. He saw our piper's fingers. He saw the melted snow coming down the mountains, turning and following the carved paths, as tears might flow down an old one's face. He saw that the grave of his many grandparents was now the grave of his father.

He had been in Paris long enough that he could sketch the curls of each of her streets, and yet it took little time for him to know, again, the smaller gnarl in the rowan tree where *Buachaille Etive Beag* first slopes up from *Lochan na Fola*. He quickly remembered the colours of the stones beneath the water of the Coe, the drawn pace of the waves upon the shores. He knew the wavering shape of the entrance to the cave of Oisín, high up in *Aonach Dubh*, as the mists passed across it.

Soon after his return in 1650, he married the daughter of our kinsman Alasdair Buidhe MacDonald, the fourteenth chief of the MacDonalds of Keppoch. She was the niece of Angus MacDonald of Achnancoichean, too, the very man who had died alongside Alasdair's father fighting against the Campbells, and she came to live with Alasdair in his house at Polveig, by Loch Leven. There, they kept a steady fire for visitors to the glen, and received clansmen and clanswomen who requested justice or aid.

There, as well, Alasdair MacIain and Lady Glen Coe often spent evenings with their *duine uasal*, known by your tongue as tacksmen. These men were Alasdair's cousins, the grandsons of *Iain Dubh*, Black John, nephew of our seventh chief. Alasdair could call upon four of them, and they were his lieutenants in every battle, every foray. For most of the while, however, they served as his gentry, taking care of each of the farms, paying their rents to their chief.

The first of the tacksmen was Alexander MacDonald of Achtriachtan, son of the eldest son of Black John. The MacDonalds of Achtriachtan were the principal family of Glen Coe, beside the family of MacIain himself, for their lands not only encompassed their namesake meadow and loch in the southeast of the glen, but also the field of Achnacon, with its cattle and village stretching toward the northwest, where the Coe gathered strength.

Farther north, and farther west, lived MacDonald of Inverrigan, the only one of the tacksmen whose first name has been forgotten. Inverrigan resided within his woods, by his stream, and though fewer of our people abided there, there were several families who took their water from *Allt Fhiodan*, and knew the dark of the shade at daybreak.

To the south lay the lands of Alexander MacDonald of Dalness, in Glen Etive, which begins beneath the arrow peak of *Buachaille Etive Mòr* and then follows the pebbled and rocky River Etive for miles under the mountains, away from all things. Alexander was well esteemed, but so, too, was his younger brother *Aillean Dubh nam Fiadh*, Black Allan of the Deer, called by this name because of his talents at the hunt.

The final tacksman of Glen Coe was John MacDonald of Laroch, whose stone house sat at the western bound of our clan's lands, where the River Laroch flows into Loch Leven across from the burial isle, where the village of Ballachulish would come to be. One story, which is still recounted in the glen and elsewhere about the Highlands, best tells of John.

Together with Big Archibald MacPhail and a few other Glen Coe men, John once went north and east into Strathspey, where he and the others relieved the chief of Clan Grant of some cattle he surely would not need. They left with a great number, heading back toward Glen Coe, and stopped for the night beside a loch. Soon, however, several of the Grants, led by their chief's son, appeared upon the hill.

John walked up to the Grant's son, holding his sword by the point, the hilt dragging upon the ground as though he were about to surrender. But at the last moment, he flipped the sword into the air, grasped it at the hilt, and struck down Grant in one blow. Seeing this, the Grants fled, and the MacDonalds went back to driving the cattle home.

After a time, however, John came to worry. He knew that he had not killed Grant immediately, and yet Grant had been left there, with no one to treat his wounds. John could not let

Grant die like that, so he left the others and returned to the lochside, where he found Grant still alive. John filled his own shoe with fresh water for Grant, and began walking.

Grant proceeded to shoot him with a pistol. Now John lay bleeding, his thigh bone smashed, while Grant lay bleeding just several paces away. They both gritted their teeth, and gasped as they tried to bring themselves up.

After several moments, John suggested that they continue the fight, and of course Grant agreed. John struggled to stand, but he could not. Grant, in the meanwhile, had recovered sufficiently that he could stand upon both feet. Grant knew that he could kill John with one stroke if he wished, but he would not so take advantage of a man, and thus he proposed friendship instead. John was taken to the home of the Grants, where was he given hospitality for a full year, recovering completely from his wound.

John's younger brother, too, was trusted by our chief Alasdair MacIain. His name was Ranald, and he was known quite as well as John.

Several years earlier, while Alasdair MacIain was yet in Paris, young Ranald had been with the rest of his clansmen fighting against the English and Lowland opponents of our King Charles I. An Englishman was taken prisoner, and soon learned that Highlanders had not been trained to fight with a sword alone, but with a sword and shield together. Quite sure that a man would require a shield only because he needed to conceal his inferiority at swordsmanship, he boasted that, armed only with a sword, he could defeat any Highlander who bore both sword and shield.

Ranald heard this and spoke to him in his language: "Man, do you think any Highlander would take such an advantage in fighting you?" Ranald said he would only fight if he gave the advantage to the Englishman, and thus he insisted that his opponent be allowed to fight with a sword, while Ranald would only have his shield and his large knife, known as a dirk.

The Englishman agreed, but Ranald's cousin of Dalness, Black Allan of the Deer, came over. Allan not only was known for his skills at the hunt, but was considered to be the finest swordsman in the whole of the army, and he offered to take Ranald's place, to meet the Englishman on equal terms. Yet Ranald refused, and prepared to fight.

It was then that Allan turned away from the Englishman, looked at Ranald and said: *'S fearr an claidheamh gu mór na bhiodag 's an targaid. Gabh mo chomhairle, oir cha 'n 'eil fios 'de dh' eireas dhuit.* (The sword is much better than the dirk. Take my advice, or there is no knowing what may happen to you.)

Ranald responded: *Cha 'n 'eil fios 'de dh' eireas dhomhsa ach eiridh an diabhull fein dhasan.* (There is no knowing what may happen to me, but the very devil will happen to him.)

The Englishman swung his sword, practicing and showing to all, and then readied. Ranald gripped a dirk in one hand, a shield in the other. They circled, I am sure, for a number of moments before they met, and the thing ended with the Englishman upon the ground. From that time, the brother of Laroch was known as *Raonull na Sgéithe*: Ranald of the Shield.

For all of these stories of fighting, Alasdair MacIain's

tacksmen provided him with counsel, for the greater part. There were many times, during his first years as our chief, when Achtriachtan, Inverrigan, Dalness and Laroch sat with Alasdair by the hearth at Polveig and weighed the news of events, not just in the Highlands and the Isles, but also in the Lowlands and in England.

They were not surprised, of course, by the Campbell's newly found support for Charles II, the son of our King Charles I. The execution of King Charles I by Oliver Cromwell and his Puritan allies in 1649 was so unpopular in Scotland that Campbell would have courted his ruin if he had stood to his principles, and this he was congenitally unable to do. In June of 1650, Charles II landed in Scotland.

Neither were Alasdair MacIain and his tacksmen surprised when, just a few weeks later, Cromwell invaded Scotland, having left to his generals the remaining task of crushing the people of Ireland. Highlander was divided from Lowlander, however, and the English won victory upon victory until, by the close of 1651, the country was under their thumb. English troops were garrisoned at Inverlochy, just twelve miles from Glen Coe.

Even so, Cromwell's rule over England came to be nearly as unpopular as his rule over Scotland and Ireland, and within two years of his death, in the summer of 1660, Charles II was crowned king of all three countries. There were great celebrations throughout England and in many of the parts of Scotland, while in Edinburgh, the Campbell was executed for his collaborations with Cromwell. The fort at Inverlochy, near us, was demolished, and the English troops were ordered away.

For the next quarter of a century, the MacDonalds of Glen Coe accepted Charles II as our king, out of expedience rather than loyalty, just as we had accepted his father and his grandfathers. To our satisfaction, indeed, Charles tread more lightly within the Highlands and the Isles than had been expected, handling matters through his Privy Council in Edinburgh. The members of the council did not leave us to ourselves, of course, for they could rely upon Campbell's chastened son Archibald, the new Earl of Argyll, to police and conquer in the name of good order. Yet for all of the clan battles of these years, for all of the territorial clamouring, the king and his council brought no armies onto our lands.

Perhaps they held back only because they were rather occupied with the king's many opponents in England and the Lowlands. Charles' younger brother James was next in line to the throne, as Charles had no legitimate children, and James' adherence to the Catholic faith raised a very outcry among so many of the English and the Lowlanders. A Catholic, it was said, would follow the Pope in Rome rather than recognise the authority of Parliament. He would ally himself with Catholic France and Spain, long the enemies of England. Popery was the root of tyranny, it was said, and Charles' conduct intimated that he was quite as much of a papist as his younger brother and heir.

So it was that when Charles died in 1685, the new King James faced suspicion, and scorn, in much of England and the Lowlands. You may know from your school days that just three years later, in 1688, James was deposed, and his Protestant daughter Mary came to the throne with her husband

Willem van Oranje, a Dutchman who was quite suddenly known in Somerset and Lincolnshire as William of Orange. The English and their textbooks call it the "Glorious Revolution."

William and Mary had no interest in coming north, and so the loyal Archibald Campbell, 10th Earl of Argyll, went south to London and handed them the throne of Scotland. Presenting the crown with him was John Dalrymple, a nobleman from the southwestern Lowlands who hoped that Scotland might unify with England, thus progressing at last into the modern era. The chief obstacles to greater Britain's betterment, Dalrymple was steadfastly convinced, were those Celts of her northwest, with our backward ways and primitive loyalties, our undeserved pride. Only when the Highlanders were brought to heel would England accept Scotland as a nation worthy of her.

By Loch Leven, far from Dalrymple and London, Alasdair MacIain sat with Achtriachtan, Inverrigan, Dalness and Laroch, and there they set upon their course: They would fight against William and return James to the throne.

The people of Glen Coe were not Catholic, but as Episcopalians, we held to many of the old Church's beliefs, far more than did the Puritans in England or the Presbyterians in the Lowlands. Yet religion was a secondary care to us, as it was to most of the Highlanders who were readying their arms against William. Among the clans declaring their support for King James were Catholics, Episcopalians, and Presbyterians alike.

No, Alasdair and his tacksmen joined the rebellion because William's reign surely would mean yet more meddling from the south, yet more incursions of English words and cannon, yet more Campbell power. James, on the other hand, had tread even more lightly in the Highlands than had his older brother Charles, and now was pledging his loyalty to the clans. Too, he was a Scottish king in the end, not a Dutch one.

Perhaps, the people of Glen Coe hoped, a restored King James would show us the richest favour of all. Perhaps we could rest, soon, knowing that our grandchildren's children would live as Gaels.

CHAPTER 19

THE OLD ROAD

I sat down for breakfast at the Clachaig Inn: Oatmeal and fruit, Café Americano because they didn't do regular coffee, scrambled eggs and baked beans and sausage. Penny and I had driven into Glencoe last night, in a coming and going drizzle.

Penny was sleeping in, and so there was room to lay out our map on the table. Last night we'd just followed the road signs, but now I could tell I was sitting near the middle of the glen. And that looming cliff, out the window, had to be *Aonach Dubh*, and that mountain to its right had to be *An t-Sron*, but then again the map said this wasn't a mountain at all—it was only a temporary rise on the way to *Bidean nam Bian*, which lay above in the distance, or so the map said, on the other side of those mists. And out the other window was another mountain, cleft almost all the way up, and it just had to be *Sgorr nam Fiannaidh*. The accents around me were Scottish, often, and English, too, but I didn't hear any Americans or Canadians or Australians.

Then I looked up and saw Penny walking toward me. The receptionist had come to our door with a message on a sheet of paper, and Penny handed it to me.

It said: Call Alistair MacDonald.

So breakfast ended quickly, and Penny snagged some food on her way back to the room. I went to the pay phone, put in some pence, and dialed the number. Ring. He's probably home. Ring. But if not, I'll just reach him a little later. Ring.

"Hello," he answered. "Alistair MacDonald."

"Hello, Mr. MacDonald, this is Ryan Littrell, calling from the Clachaig Inn."

"Yes."

"Well, we just got in last night, and I wanted to thank you for responding to my email, you know, and we're just looking forward to being here for the next week or so."

"Maybe you would like to come visit us."

"Sure, that would be just great. That would be great. Like I said, we'll be here for the next week or so, and we don't have anything planned, so we can stop by anytime. When would be a good day for you?"

"Now."

"Oh, OK, absolutely. It'll take us a little bit to get ready, but we could be there pretty quickly."

I could almost hear him grinning. "No, you should take your time. I don't mean to rush you. We'll be here all day. You'll be going along the old road, then?"

I didn't know the old road from the Silk Road, but I said yes.

He was grinning again. "You'll be going out the back of the Clachaig, then, and follow that road along the Coe. It will take you across the old bridge into Glencoe village." He told me just where we could find his and Rosalin's house.

All right, OK, good. I hung up, checked for change, didn't have any, headed back to the room to make sure Penny was all right with the new plan for the day.

That took me by the front desk, where I heard the receptionist say to someone on the phone, "Aye, good, I'll pass it on." Then the receptionist saw me, and motioned me over.

"Well, wait, Mr. MacDonald," she said on the phone, "here he is just now." She handed it to me.

"Hello, is this Ryan?"

"Yes, hello."

"Lachie MacDonald here. How do you do?"

"Oh, hello, doing well, how are you?"

"I'm well, Ryan, thank you. Now, I know you've been in contact with my wife Diane about the DNA, and that's just splendid. We'll be able to meet this week up in Glencoe, yes?"

"Yes, absolutely."

"Well, we look forward to it. Now, listen, we have a good friend who lives in Ballachulish, and you might know that's not far west of the Clachaig there. We spoke to him, oh, just a wee bit ago, and he said he would be happy to take you across to the burial isle in his boat while you're about. Might you be interested in that?"

I'm sure I said something that sounded like a grateful yes.

So, soon, we had a plan. Today was Monday, and Penny and I would meet Lachie's friend Robert Watt at the loch on Friday morning. Lachie and Diane would see us when we got back to shore.

And a little while after saying bye to Lachie and hanging

up, I stepped outside with Penny. *Sgorr nam Fiannaidh* began rising right there, right on the other side of those picnic tables, and several more steps beyond that, it was already rocky and steep. In the distance, streams of rainwater were coming down *Aonach Dubh* and *An t-Sron*. All around in the air was this cold vapor, in every breath, like I'd just stepped out of a cool shower. Even now, in late October, much of the green in the trees and grass was still there, among all the reds and golds and rock.

We drove down the old road, with trees beside us all the way. The left side sloped down toward the river, and the right side sloped up into mountains. I tried not to notice that sign depicting falling rocks. The road was narrow enough that I slowed down when a car approached, and so did that other car, and we all gave a thanks-for-that wave. Now the river was just to our left, with red leaves on the banks. We crossed the bridge, slowly, into the village.

Things were quiet here, and we didn't see anyone. When we closed the car doors, it sounded loud. The village seemed to be made of one street, along with a few side roads here and there, and it looked like there might be just a few dozen houses, some of them white and some of them stone-gray, with slate shingles and beds of purple and blue flowers beside them, and tended green hedges. Near the center of the street stood the village's church, its steeple looking out over the highest house around. And on every side, out there, above, were the mountains and the hills.

We were pretty sure this house was the right one, so we walked up and knocked, and after a moment Rosalin answered the door. "Welcome, welcome, please come in," she said, smiling.

Alexander, her and Alistair's son, was standing behind her, and he shook our hands and said hello. The two of them brought us in, and asked whether we might like to sit in the living room, and offered us something to eat or drink, but no, we said, we've already had breakfast, thank you. "Alistair will be by in just a moment," said Rosalin.

In the living room, we talked about our flight, about the drive up from Edinburgh to the Clachaig. After several minutes, the door opened and Alistair came in, and he welcomed us and walked over to his chair. He stayed silent while the rest of us finished talking about how the winters had gotten wetter around here recently. Then we were all quiet for a few seconds.

"I want to be DNA'd," said Alistair.

"All right, excellent," I responded.

Brundage, my Canadian cousin, had visited Alistair and Rosalin in Glencoe several times, and my New Zealand cousin Colin had come by, too, years before. Alexander, the genealogist in Alistair and Rosalin's family, had looked into Colin's family tree, and believed that Colin really was descended from Donald, the younger brother of the 14th chief, just as Colin claimed. And it turned out that my cousin Lachie's friend, Robert Watt, was married to Rosalin's sister Jeanette. Robert, who'd be taking us to the burial isle in a few days, was Alistair's brother-in-law.

Now Alexander laid out a few documents. He'd spent hundreds of hours uncovering the history of the Glencoe

MacDonalds, traveling to libraries and looking through old records. As I sat on the couch, Alistair noticed the book in my hand, the scruffed one with black ink underlines and notes in the margins. It was called *The MacDonalds of Glencoe*, and I'd been reading it for weeks, trying to find clues.

"Sander, he has your book," said Alistair.

Alexander's documents showed that he and Alistair were patrilineally descended from Donald MacDonald, who was born in about 1770 in Glencoe, and married Ann MacDonald of Kilmonivaig Parish, about thirty miles to the northeast. This Donald was definitely not the same man as Colin's ancestor Donald.

Alexander didn't know who his ancestor Donald's parents were, but his family always said that their MacDonald ancestors were in the glen long before 1770. Alexander even had a hunch that Donald might have been descended from the tacksmen of Achtriachtan, in the southeast part of the glen. From his book, I knew that the tacksmen of Glencoe in the 17th and 18th centuries were the chief's paternal cousins, his lieutenants, and that the tacksmen of Achtriachtan had been placed in charge of more lands and people than any of the others.

The five of us sat by the fireplace, looking through papers and books while the rain outside came and went, and after an hour or so, Alexander brought in tea and sweetbreads and cookies for us. Alistair talked about his childhood here in the village, about his years working beside the mountains, and his years climbing up into them. A twinkle came to his eye when he spoke of their Glencoe Heritage Trust, their purchase of the old clan lands. Alexander held his cup of tea, cautious, scholarly, leaning in to read old handwriting and then sitting back again, answering each question only as far as it could be rightly answered.

And Rosalin prodded some memories, and deferred sometimes, and other times said no, not quite. When I asked about her family history, she mentioned that her mother's maiden name was Rankin. Her family had long been in the glen, too, just like Alistair's. She was descended from Duncan Rankin, and that name rang a bell. "Aye, well, he was the first one killed, wasn't he?" she said.

Among all these notes and records was a list of people named MacDonald who left Scotland in the 18th and 19th centuries. The list had been compiled by Clan Donald, and it encompassed MacDonalds from all over Scotland, not just from Glencoe. Penny and I skipped to "McDonald, Angus"—the name of my ancestor, the man who'd been discovered through the Warren County, Kentucky records and the DNA match with Jim McDonald of Houston. But there were so many Angus McDonalds listed here, and not one was tied to Glencoe.

Still, Penny and I went through the list and wrote down a few candidates, the ones who might be *my* Angus McDonald, or at least might be related to him. We saw that all four of the Angus McDonalds who fit the bill were men who happened to end up in Virginia before 1775, and that made me wonder. My Angus died in Kentucky in the late 1820s, and many of the people who went to Kentucky in the late 1700s and early 1800s went there from Virginia. Was my Angus one of these

MacDonalds who emigrated to Virginia before the American Revolution?

One of us looked at the clock right about then, and we all realized we'd been sitting here talking for more than five hours—dusk would be coming on in a bit. We said our good-byes and thank-yous, and as Penny and I walked out the door, Alistair mentioned that he'd send away for his cheek swab soon.

Back at the Clachaig, Penny and I took our seats in the pub, with our pre-dinner pints and all these pages of notes and copied documents. I thought again about Alexander's suspicion that he and Alistair might be patrilineally descended from the tacksmen of Achtriachtan. Taking what I knew about my cousin Colin's ancestry, I mapped out the Glencoe MacDonald family tree, or at least the *men's* family tree, with the chiefs on the left and the tacksmen's families on the right:

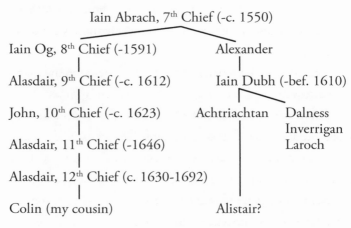

Iain Abrach, 7th Chief (-c. 1550)

Iain Og, 8th Chief (-1591)   Alexander

Alasdair, 9th Chief (-c. 1612)   Iain Dubh (-bef. 1610)

John, 10th Chief (-c. 1623)   Achtriachtan   Dalness
     Inverrigan
Alasdair, 11th Chief (-1646)   Laroch

Alasdair, 12th Chief (c. 1630-1692)

Colin (my cousin)   Alistair?

Now that I could see Alistair's possible connection to Colin, I began to wonder whether I was descended from one of the tacksmen's families myself. Colin and Uncle Chuck had recently tested another thirty DNA markers—beyond the thirty-seven markers already tested—and the two of them only matched on sixty-two out of the combined total of sixty-seven. This gave us even stronger evidence of what the thirty-seven marker results had suggested: Chuck's line, my line, probably broke off from Colin's line before the 17th century, but after the 15th. What if the split happened right *there*, at the top of this chart, where Iain Og gave rise to the chiefs (and Colin) while his younger brother Alexander gave rise to the tacksmen (and Chuck)?

If my ancestor Angus McDonald emigrated to the American colonies before the Revolutionary War, then he'd fit the profile—I knew from several books that many Highland emigrants to America at the time were tacksmen and their families. Alexander's book gave hints, too, telling of the younger brother of some tacksman who disappeared from the records, and of sons whose names were known, but whose stories had been lost.

And for the next few days, Penny and I went to the places in the glen where my Angus might have been born.

At Achtriachtan, there was just one house, down and away from the main road, and it was beside a loch. The ground sloped up quickly, right at the edge of this field, and now the rocks were jutting up, almost on every side, ascending and ascending until you could barely see them anymore in the sky. Only when the mists passed for a moment would you notice that the crumbling, up there, is what you see near the peaks of cathedrals.

At Laroch, now part of the town of Ballachulish, you could smell the sea by the old slate quarry, and the river was rushing and pouring under the stone bridge, and tree branches arched up and then almost dipped their ends down into the water. Up above the town, up on *Beinn Bhàn*, the sun was shining, but farther up and beyond, out on the top of *Sgorr Bhàn*, the gray was already moving across. Stone fences began at the town's edge and extended up toward the mountains, showing where one family's land had once ended, and another's had begun.

At Dalness, though, no one seemed to have lived, ever, because it lay so far away from the main road, away from where anyone else was going, and there were no signs of where houses might once have been. These mountains had their own river to rise up from, with stones sticking up at first, dry above the trickle, and then disappearing below when the water built.

We came to Inverrigan, then, nearly by accident. We were leaving the Glencoe Visitor Centre, a museum run by the National Trust for Scotland, and Alexander's book said that Inverrigan had been somewhere, not far, to our northwest, and so we walked beyond the little parking lot, toward those trees. There we found a path leading into the woods.

The path was narrow, and all around were old trees without their leaves, sticking up into the air like spines. We could barely see the sky behind those birds' nests. Then the way almost cleared for a bit, so that the peak of *Sgorr na Cìche* lay up there in its fog.

But soon we were walking into thick woods again, and

after a few minutes, we saw the stones. That's when it began raining. That's when we stopped and stood.

The stones had once been packed together, making up the walls of someone's house, but now they were just a foot or two high, with their collapsings all around. Even after all the years, though, they made a rectangle, not much bigger than a living room. Grass grew where the floor had been, and plants and flowers grew around the walls. There was moss in the mortar.

No one was here, and the water was coming down hard. We walked up to it. In the middle of the house, on the ground, was a wooden cross. Nine trees had been planted outside the house, each protected by an enclosing fence.

Here, and at Achtriachtan and Laroch and Dalness, I would look over and see nothing, and then look behind me and see nothing, but that just couldn't be right, because it seemed like someone was watching. Everywhere, the mountains stood over us, and soon they felt like shelter.

Still, Friday came quickly, and after breakfast we drove to the loch, to where my cousin Lachie had said to go. And there was Robert Watt.

He smiled, said hello, and shook our hands. "Now, you'll need these," he said. "It can get very slippery out there." He handed us life vests, waterproof overalls, and knee-high rain boots.

He led us down to the dock, and we stepped into his boat. We were just above the surface of the loch, like it was a pool and we were standing in it. From down here, the mountains reached higher, all around, taking up even more of the sky. The engine started, the mists began coming down from the mountains, the drizzle started again.

There were three small ports on the isle, I'd heard, one for each of the local clans. We were silent as the boat started moving, and the dock passed behind us. "Robert," I asked, "are we going to the MacDonald port?"

"Aye," he said.

CHAPTER 20

NA SEUMASAICH

Nuair a chruinnich na fineachan, cha robh cus a' cromadh an cinn.

When the clans gathered, there were few bowed heads.

The chiefs and their men had agreed to meet here, upon the field called Dalcomera beside the River Lochy, in May of 1689. Our King James had fled England after being deposed by the usurpers William and Mary, but had gone safely to our cousins the Irish, who had just now proclaimed him their king, as well. With James advancing from Dublin into the north of Ireland, where English and Lowlanders had settled, it was time for Highlanders to come out. All of the clans who had pledged their loyalty to James marched to the place. Every piper played the music of war, and we were soon called *Na Seumasaich.*

"Jacobites," in your tongue.

Here, at Dalcomera, stood the MacDonalds from the southern parts of the Isle of Skye, whose boats rightly caught the winds, and the MacDonalds of Glen Garry, who well knew the highest peaks of Kintail and the quiet forests of

Bunloinn and Inchnacardoch. Here stood the MacDonalds of Keppoch, who never shied from a proper foray, and the MacDonalds of Clan Ranald, whose call reached from the outermost isles into the mainland.

Here were the Camerons, led by their great-hearted chief Ewen Cameron, and the MacLeans from the green Isle of Mull, who had withstood the invasions and sieges of the Campbells. Here, among so many of the others, were the Frasers who lived about Loch Ness, the MacLeods from the winding peninsulas of northern Skye, the Grants and the Mac-Lachlans, the Stewarts and the MacAulays, the MacAlisters of Kintyre, and the outlawed MacGregors.

Here, too, were the MacDonalds of Glen Coe. There were barely more than one hundred of us, but our Alasdair Mac-Iain was esteemed by the clans as though he commanded an army. He was an older man now, with white hair that came down far, and yet he had the same eyes, and the same voice, that he had when he returned to his people from Paris, almost forty years before. He still stood six feet, seven inches tall, with the same shoulders. Beside him were his sons, while his tacksmen remained close by: MacDonald of Achtriachtan, of Inverrigan, of Dalness and of Laroch.

This army was led by James Graham, Viscount Dundee, who would come to be known as Bonnie Dundee. He was daring, resourceful at each turn, trusted by his king and re-spected by all of the chiefs, so that the rivalries among them receded. More Highlanders quickly declared their loyalty to James, although a few chiefs, not the Campbell alone, profit-ed from William's new government and so decided to support it.

Just weeks after the gathering at Dalcomera, Dundee and the loyal clansmen went southeast and took Blair Castle, and on the 27th of July, the government forces marched from the south to confront us. The government army was nearly 4,000 strong, led by Sir Hugh Mackay, a Highlander and veteran general whose clan once had been loyal to James and his family.

At Blair Castle, Bonnie Dundee convened his war council, listening to each of his commanders. Their men had been on a quick, fatiguing march, and the government army was fully a third larger, with more food, provisions and horses besides.

Therefore remain here and rest our men, advised his regular officers, the career military men who had come from all parts. Pare down the government army, gradually, in the hope of gaining the advantage in the near future, but do not risk so great a loss with tired soldiers.

No, urged Alasdair MacIain and the other Highland chiefs: Attack now and shock them, for our men are not nearly so fatigued as your officers suppose, and they are not afraid. Our spirits will rise only when we fight. Ewen Cameron, chief of the Clan Cameron, said that he could not promise a victory if the cautious path were taken, but "be assured, my Lord, that if we are fairly engaged, we will either lose our army, or carry a complete victory...and I have still observed that when I fought under the greatest disadvantage of numbers, I still had the greatest victories."

Bonnie Dundee chose whole-heartedly to fight, and he

insisted upon leading the attack himself. Knowing that the government army would have to march through a particular pass in order to reach Blair Castle, the Highlanders rushed to that place, known as Killiecrankie, and so were able to take a commanding position on the hill above.

The MacDonalds of Glen Coe were on the right flank, with the MacDonalds of Clan Ranald and Glen Garry, when Mackay and his army arrived and formed their battle lines below. The government forces began firing their muskets up the hill, rapidly at first and then only occasionally, as the Highlanders waited for the proper time.

At seven o'clock the advance began, and Bonnie Dundee stood before his army and said, "Remember that today begins the fate of your king, your religion and your country. Behave yourselves, therefore, as true Scotsmen, and let us, by this action, redeem the credit of our nation, which is laid low by the treacheries and cowardice of some of its countrymen."

The Gaels marched, while the government's bullets came into us, once and again, killing dozens and soon hundreds. None fled. We kept marching, as more of our clansmen fell, and marched on while yet more fell, and yet more. But now the Highland men were near enough to let loose one volley from our muskets, and then we threw the guns to the ground, took our swords into our hands, and charged.

We crashed into the government line, sending William's servants into a retreat, or to the ground. Everywhere, all along the line, the redcoats collapsed and fled within minutes, unable even to summon a hope at matching us, man to man. Most of their army lay upon this field, with Mackay scrambling away.

Still, even as the redcoats disappeared to their south and their east, even as the pipes began the tunes of praise and remembrance, Bonnie Dundee lay dying. He had charged with the rest, and was among those hundreds who fell to the government's muskets. He was brought, in plaids, to the churchyard near Blair Castle.

Several days later, after his messengers had gone all the way to London, William was given the news of Killiecrankie, and shortly was asked whether he might wish to send reinforcements north to Scotland. He replied: "Armies are needless; the war is over with Dundee's life."

Thus, William's good servant Mackay quickly wrote to the Highland chiefs, offering them a full pardon if they only would give their loyalty to their rightful sovereigns William and Mary. He sent his letter along, and waited with confidence.

After a few days, his messenger brought him the response from the chiefs. He held the letter in his hands and broke the seal. It read: "That you may know the sentiments of men of honour, we declare to you and all the world that we scorn your usurper....We will all die with our swords in our hands before we fail in our loyalty and sworn allegiance to our sovereign."

Despite even their defeat at Dunkeld a few weeks later, the chiefs did not waver. Autumn was upon them, however, and after a whole summer at arms, without farming or fattening, they needed to prepare for the coming winter. They agreed to part ways for now, pledging to rise for James when called.

They paused, too, because their main army was yet in Ireland with James himself, and a final victory there would turn the tide in Scotland, allowing our king to bring his full power to the Highlands. But the victory would not come during this autumn of 1689, for the two armies remained at a stalemate in County Louth throughout September and October before retreating to their headquarters for the winter.

So it was that Alasdair MacIain and his clansmen made our way home in October with our neighbours and kinsmen of Keppoch. The MacDonalds found ourselves passing through the country of the Campbells of Glen Orchy and Glen Lyon, and took the opportunity to unburden the traitors of some cattle, horses, and sheep. We felt no pangs of conscience, after all of those centuries in which the Campbells plundered with lawyers and pilfered with politics. Taking from a thief is no thievery at all. Soon, we were back in the glen, as the cold arrived and Alasdair and his tacksmen awaited word of the rebellion's course.

Perhaps, during that winter, Alasdair learned of the new drills at Perth, roughly ninety miles away. Straw-filled dummies were being stabbed by bayonets. Archibald Campbell, the Earl of Argyll, had graciously offered to create a regiment that would answer to William and Mary, and the government in Edinburgh had blessed this act of public service. The Lowland authorities had been so impressed with His Lordship's selflessness that they had given their approval even before Campbell's arrival, in London, to hand William and Mary the throne of Scotland.

Already there were five hundred soldiers in this Royal Regiment bunkered at Perth, and like Englishmen, like the troops we had felled at Killiecrankie, they wore red. While most of the ordinary men were tenants from Campbell lands in the southern Highlands, their officers were veteran Lowlanders and Campbell gentry, who even now were forging a modern, efficient unit.

Once a month, standing in formation, the soldiers were read aloud William's laws. Once a month, they heard: "If any shall presume to beat or abuse his host, or the wife, child or servant of his host where he is quartered, he shall be put in irons for it."

CHAPTER 21

BACK TO THE SECOND MACIAIN

In Robert's boat, droplets started collecting on our hair, and Penny and I could hear the quiet motor and the water sloshing behind us. All three of us stayed silent. The wind was cold in our faces, and the waves were weak, for now, and the boat bobbed up and down just a little while going forward. We were the only ones on the loch.

Out ahead of us, the isle was blurred by all the drizzle, and from here, most of the trees seemed to have changed their colors. Now we were drawing closer, though, and I could make out some green leaves and the wet grass, and I could see how the first few feet of the isle, right above the surface of the loch, were moss and rock. And there on the hill, sticking up like bottom teeth, were gravestones.

We slowed down, drifting for a little, and soon we were floating into the MacDonald port. It was a pebbled beach, just a few yards across.

We walked on slippery grass and rocks, stepped around little pools. Then we climbed up this short slope, and there were the first gravestones. Most were from the 19th century, with some from the early 20th. They were dark gray, made from the slate of Ballachulish.

This one was placed by Alexander McKenzie in memory of his wife Isabella McColl, who died at the age of thirty-three, and their daughter Ann, who died at the age of three days. It read: "My glass has run, Yours is running, Be wise in time, Your hour is coming." There was an Alexander McKenzie who lay over here, maybe the same Alexander McKenzie, with a stone that said: "He was honest in business, much respected by all who knew him."

Then I saw that name for the first time: "Angus McDonald, Tacksman of Inverrigan, and his wife Mary Rankin, by order of their son Allan McDonald." And nearby we found this: "Alexander McDonald, Hereditary Henchman to the Chief of the McDonalds of Glencoe, and Gardener on the Estate for 40 yrs."

We walked slowly, watching our steps, wondering. We stopped and bent over to read. After a bit, we found: "Angus McDonald, tenant, formerly in Achtriachtan, d. 20 Feb. 1786 aged 67 yrs." The gravestones didn't stand in ordered rows, but fit where they could, wherever there wasn't a rocky outcrop or the near-surface roots of an old tree. Robert took us to the stones he knew, and told some of the stories he knew. A few minutes later, we saw: "Angus McDonald, son of Alexander McDonald of Dalness, who d. 22 Apr. 1794 aged 80 yrs."

And among all of them were the stones that said things like: *Tha n leachd so air suidheachadh n so le Domhnuill Mac-Coinnich saor ann so n Laraich mar chuimhneachan air a mhn aoidh Mairi nicRaing chaocheal beatha anns a chair nich air*

189

XXII do'n mhairt MDCCCXXXVIII.

Another one read: *Tha n cuimhneachan so air a chur a suas leis a bhantraich Caorstan nic an t-soar agus a chuild eile don teaghlach aig am an dol an air chuirt do dh Australia 1852.* I ran my hands across the words, like they were in Braille.

Only then did we notice the burial vault, off to the side, looking across the loch to the mainland. It had three short walls, forming three sides of a rectangle, and one side rose up into a gable, so that the burial vault looked like a little house whose roof had fallen away with one of its walls. We walked to it and saw the inscription: "Burial Place of MacDonald of Glencoe."

"Underneath this," Robert said, "is the crypt. That's where all of the chiefs and their families are buried, going back to the second MacIain."

He and Penny walked off to other graves. I stepped out to the edge of the isle, looked out at the houses and mountains on the mainland, came back to the crypt, and now Robert's voice was muffled, almost distant, and Penny's was, too.

I placed my hand on the wall of the little house. The wind was coming through the long grass and the leaves in the trees, and the water was hitting the rocks below. I bent my head down and closed my eyes. I could hear my breath. Hopefully, nobody was watching me. I said it just once, and said it silently.

I will find you.

Soon I could hear Robert and Penny's voices coming closer, and they didn't even look at me like I was crazy. I'd told myself no, I wouldn't do it, but when Robert asked whether

I'd like to have a picture taken of me beside the burial vault, I said OK, fine. And as he pointed the camera at me, and I clasped my hands, I didn't feel like an intruder. It didn't seem like I was posing in someone else's family photo.

The three of us stepped away, back down to the port, and we pushed off. The engine started again. Penny and I looked back and saw the isle getting smaller and smaller behind us, while the glen became bigger and bigger before us.

Back on shore, rain gear off, we walked to our cars. Robert told us how to get to the coffee shop, where we'd soon have the pleasure of meeting Dr. Lachlan MacDonald, dentist of Paisley, a large town outside Glasgow.

Last night, sitting at the Clachaig Inn, I'd received an email from the DNA company saying that, like Uncle Chuck and my New Zealand cousin Colin, Lachie MacDonald of Paisley had gotten another thirty DNA markers tested, beyond the original thirty-seven. Clicking through, I'd discovered that Chuck and Lachie matched perfectly on all thirty of the new markers; Chuck matched Lachie on sixty-five out of sixty-seven markers, but only matched Colin on sixty-two out of sixty-seven. That meant my line probably branched off from Lachie's line between the early 17th century and the mid-18th century, more than a century after my line branched off from Colin's.

All right, back to the Glencoe family tree:

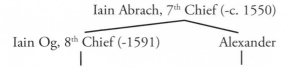

Iain Abrach, 7th Chief (-c. 1550)

Iain Og, 8th Chief (-1591)   Alexander

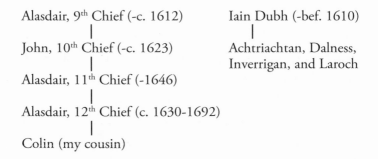

Alasdair, 9th Chief (-c. 1612)   Iain Dubh (-bef. 1610)

John, 10th Chief (-c. 1623)   Achtriachtan, Dalness, Inverrigan, and Laroch

Alasdair, 11th Chief (-1646)

Alasdair, 12th Chief (c. 1630-1692)

Colin (my cousin)

A few days ago, after visiting Alistair, Rosalin and their son Alexander, I'd suspected that my ancestor Angus McDonald of Garrard County, Kentucky was patrilineally descended from one of those four tacksmen on the right side, and now, just maybe, there was a way to find out whether that could be true. Since Lachie only matched Colin on sixty-three out of sixty-seven markers, it was likely that their two lines branched off from one another in the 16th or 17th centuries, which meant that Lachie very well could be a descendant of one of the tacksmen. And if he *was*, then I was probably descended from one of them, too, because of how closely Lachie matched Uncle Chuck.

So, walking up to the place called *Crafts and Things* with Robert and Penny, I wondered whether I was about to learn more from Lachie. This was an old house near the village of Glencoe, with stone walls and a slate roof, and there were crafts, and things, to be bought on the first floor. There were paintings of the loch and antiques. There were photos of the mountains. We went downstairs to the coffee shop, found a table, and soon the three of them were joining us.

Jeanette, Robert's wife, was first down the steps, shaking

our hands and welcoming us. I could see the slight resemblance to her sister Rosalin. Then Diane gave us a hug, and behind her was her husband Lachie, who wanted to know all about how our trip had been coming along.

We told them about our walks around the glen, about meeting up with Alistair and Rosalin and Alexander, about life at the Clachaig Inn. "Oh," Jeanette said, "you don't have to do that. You're welcome to stay with us whenever you're here. We'd be happy to have you."

Lachie and Diane spent a lot of time in Paisley, down south, but also lived on the Isle of Lismore, near here, where Lachie had been born and raised. His parents and grandparents had always spoken Gaelic at home. His father and grandfather had been well-known Gaelic poets and songwriters, and his uncles had been, too. Lachie knew most of their poems and songs by heart. He made sure not to forget.

Since childhood, he'd known that his MacDonald ancestors were from Glencoe, and many times over the years, he'd attended the memorial service, held each February 13th. He'd climbed many of the mountains of the glen, and had sailed in and out of Loch Leven again and again, and all over the west coast of Scotland. He knew the history of the Highlands and the Isles, not just from the books on his shelves, but also from the stories he'd grown up hearing.

"Well," I said, "it looks like I'm descended from a man named Angus McDonald, and I don't know where he was born, but I know that he died in the state of Kentucky."

Pause. "That's, I don't know, a few hundred miles south of Chicago."

Yes, OK, right.

"So I figured out from some records in Missouri, which is west of Kentucky, that my ancestor Hiram McDonald was the son of John McDonald and Elizabeth Downing, and then a genealogist discovered that John McDonald lived in this particular county in Kentucky. Then a DNA match with Jim McDonald of Houston, Texas, which you all probably know about, proved that my ancestor John McDonald was the son of Angus McDonald of Kentucky."

"Well, Ryan," Lachie said, "that's great. Thank you very much for that. Now, I take it that the DNA shows that your MacDonalds were related to my MacDonalds?"

"Yes, that's right."

"Well, then, from here on out, it's just like taxes and recordkeeping, you know."

I nodded.

I also had no idea what he was talking about.

"Somewhere in my office," he continued, "there are all these files, big files, with mysterious papers in them. They're pleasant-looking, I suppose, and quite official, and very competent people have put them together. Very intelligent people. Well-regarded people. But once in a while, just once in a wee while, someone asks me to take a look at them. I start looking at the numbers, the columns and figures and such. And all's well at the beginning, as someone takes me down the rows, but after a page or two the numbers start to lose their focus. Do you know what I mean?"

I nodded.

And now I kind of had an idea what he was talking about.

"I just break out in a cold sweat, every time. The hairs stand up on the back of my neck. All of these Angus Mac-Donalds and John MacDonalds and Donald MacDonalds, and Angus son of Angus son of John son of Allan son of Angus. I think all of it is absolutely splendid, really, and I'm very happy to know that there are good people who can sort it all out, you know. But if you don't mind, I'd rather pull teeth."

Luckily, his cousin John had compiled their family tree. It was all on one large sheet of paper, like a heraldic banner. Because of its size, Lachie and Diane had left it behind at Robert and Jeanette's house nearby, where they were staying. Would we like to go there?

Sure, yes, that would be great.

At the house, just down the road, we were welcomed in, and Robert and Jeanette said to make ourselves at home. We found ourselves talking and laughing for an hour, and then another hour.

But soon it was time for Lachie to ceremoniously unfurl his family tree and spread it out on the floor. We followed the generations up, from Lachie to his parents and grandparents, until we came to James MacDonald, who left Glencoe for the Isle of Lismore in the late 18th century.

James' parents weren't listed here, but there was a long line connecting him to an Angus MacDonald, who was alive in 1692. Lachie's family must have passed on the tradition that their ancestor James was descended from this Angus, who lived at Achnacon, the wide field in the center of the glen. Then we moved up one generation and saw that the father of this Angus of Achnacon was a man named Alexander

MacDonald.

The tacksman of Achtriachtan.

If Lachie's family tradition had it right, then the Glencoe tree now looked like this:

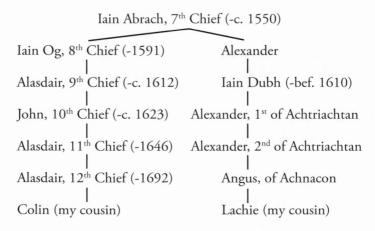

Iain Abrach, 7th Chief (-c. 1550)

Iain Og, 8th Chief (-1591) Alexander

Alasdair, 9th Chief (-c. 1612) Iain Dubh (-bef. 1610)

John, 10th Chief (-c. 1623) Alexander, 1st of Achtriachtan

Alasdair, 11th Chief (-1646) Alexander, 2nd of Achtriachtan

Alasdair, 12th Chief (-1692) Angus, of Achnacon

Colin (my cousin) Lachie (my cousin)

There was no clear proof that Lachie was patrilineally descended from Angus MacDonald of Achnacon, son of the tacksman of Achtriachtan, but family legends were often true. Especially in the Highlands. The Gaelic tradition was almost entirely oral, and genealogies were passed down from one generation to the next without ever being written down. The Lord Lyon Court of Arms in Edinburgh had recently recognized a new chief based, in part, on an oral genealogy, known as a *sloinneadh*.

One thing was clear: The DNA fit Lachie's family story. The people who'd passed on this *sloinneadh*, Lachie's grandparents and great-grandparents and great-great-grandparents, his aunts and uncles and his passed-away cousins, never could have known that every male MacDonald in their family carried something of the Glencoe chiefs in their chromosomes. But the things they had said for more than three hundred years were perfectly consistent with what the DNA was saying, now, for the first time. Based on his close-but-not-so-close DNA match with Colin, I'd suspected that Lachie was descended from one of the tacksmen's families, and suddenly I had a strong clue about which family it was.

And so, just as suddenly, I had a hint of who could have been the father, grandfather, or great-grandfather of my ancestor Angus McDonald. Was I descended from the Mac-Donalds of Achtriachtan?

Back in New York, at my computer again, I turned from the DNA and began looking for the documents, the paper trail, that might tell me more about my ancestor Angus, father of John and grandfather of Hiram. Before the trip to Glencoe, I'd discovered that my Angus left a will in Garrard County, Kentucky in 1826, and passed away by 1830. From census records and Internet posts, it appeared that my Angus was in Kentucky by the 1790s, but no one seemed to know where he lived before then.

Maybe, though, there were records at the Garrard County courthouse that would shed light on Angus' family. Online, I found Kathy Vockery, a genealogist in Garrard County, who said she'd be willing to look into the records there.

A couple of weeks later, a yellow envelope from Kathy was in my mailbox, and I opened it. Inside were several photocopied pages.

Here, on top, was Angus' will, and I looked for his signature, but then I could tell it was written in the clerk's handwriting; this was simply the court's copy. That would explain why the name was given as McDaniel, not McDonald. Reading through the lines, I saw that Angus had left all of his property to his wife Nancy.

Then the will read: "As for my first children, I have given them all that I intend for them and that I had of my own property." There, listed among the adult children who'd received all that they were going to receive, was my ancestor John. From census records, I knew that Angus and Nancy had one son together, so the phrase "my first children" meant that Nancy really wasn't the mother of John and the others, just as suspected.

Next in the envelope, after the will, was a copy of the inventory of Angus' estate; the executor had sold off much of Angus' personal property in order to help support Nancy, and the items and buyers were all listed here. The date of the estate sale was August 25, 1828, suggesting that Angus died in the spring or summer of that year—about the same time as his son John, my ancestor.

I read through the list. A cupboard full of plates, cups, knives, and forks. A looking glass, an oven. A field of standing corn. And then a "parcel of old books," sold to John B. Jennings for 62½ cents. So Angus was probably literate. He owned books that, in 1828, were considered old. Perhaps these were 18th century books he'd inherited or bought, and perhaps he'd been an educated man.

Next in the envelope was a record dated February 10, 1821. Here, set down in the clerk's handwriting, Angus informed the judge that he had a claim to a certain piece of land, and that he wanted to pass on the claim to two of his sons, in case they wished to pursue it. One son was John, my ancestor, and the other was George, the youngest, born in about 1815 to Angus and Nancy.

Angus told the judge that his uncle, also named Angus McDonald, had passed away. As a result, my Angus said, he was "entitled to a lot of land in the state of Virginia, entered, surveyed and granted to John Savage and Company for their services in the War of 1756." This was the French and Indian War, also known as the Seven Years' War, when the British and French fought for control of Canada and the lands west of the Thirteen Colonies.

Angus continued: "The said Angus McDonald, deceased, did serve in the war aforesaid and has departed this life, leaving the said Angus McDonald, the younger, his only heir resident in America."

I looked up from the page and said it back to myself. My ancestor Angus had an Uncle Angus who fought in the French and Indian War of 1756 to 1763, who was awarded land in Virginia for his service in that war, and who, apparently, died without having any heirs—or at least any heirs who lived in the United States.

The last piece of paper in this envelope from Kathy was a copy of a letter that had been written several years before, and had been sent to the Garrard County Historical Society. It had come from a man who was descended from my ancestor Angus. It was short, with an introductory sentence and then one full paragraph. It said that before Angus went to Kentucky, he and his family lived in Amherst County, Virginia.

Now I knew the path forward. If I could identify this Uncle Angus, this old veteran of the French and Indian War, I might be able to identify his brother, and identifying his brother meant identifying the father of my ancestor Angus. And if this letter to the Garrard County Historical Society had it right, then the records of Amherst County, Virginia might tell me who my Angus was, and where he'd come from.

But just before I began looking to Virginia, I got an email from the DNA company. Uncle Chuck had a new match.

This man matched Chuck more closely than anyone else did, with the exception of Jim McDonald of Houston, fellow descendant of my ancestor Angus. Besides Jim, this new match appeared to be my closest cousin.

His name was Alistair MacDonald, of Glencoe.

CHAPTER 22

BÒID NA
H-ÙMHLACHD

Fiù mus d'fhuair iad buaidh oirnn a-rithist 's a-rithist, cha robh sinne aig àird ar neirt.

Even before the defeats, we were not at our full strength.

In those first few months of 1690, while Alasdair MacIain and his tacksmen waited for word from our King James, they knew that their people could not give much more. At Killie-crankie and at Dunkeld, several months before, we had lost half of our men, so that scarcely fifty of fighting age remained.

In those winter months, so many of our children were brought into new houses to be raised with their cousins, who would come to be their brothers and sisters. In those winter months, so many mothers held their tears until the night, when the rest were asleep.

Yet, once the call came, a small party gathered beside the loch, as we had promised. Alasdair MacIain would stay behind, for now, as would his heir Iain, called John in your language. The men would be led by Alasdair's younger son, known as Alasdair Og, who had few fears.

They joined an army of Highlanders walking to Loch

Ness in April. Only 1,200 were with them, for the bitterest cold had lingered into the spring, preventing more men from leaving the fields and cattle. The clans had been assured that 8,000 troops from Ireland would arrive, but only a few officers had come. The bulk of James' army was needed there, it was said, for William himself was even now preparing to invade the Irish. The chiefs were loath to send many of their clansmen into battle while James remained in Ireland, while matters there remained so very unsettled. Some began to wonder, even, whether James was a king worthy of our swords.

Those voices gained a new force at the close of April, when James' man, Thomas Buchan, brought the small army of Highlanders to camp beside the River Spey, by the village of Cromdale. Buchan neglected to place guards by one of the river fords, and William's cavalry came to that ford in the middle of the night, while most of the Highland men were asleep.

Finding no resistance, the government's horsemen crossed the river and charged into the camp. They hacked in the darkness. The Highlanders who were not instantly killed ran up into the hills, and they, too, surely would have been struck down were it not for the mist that suddenly formed about the upper slopes. The disappearing clansmen, it later would be written, seemed "rather to be people received up into clouds than flying from an enemy."

Alasdair Og and the men of Glen Coe returned home from Cromdale, but nearly a third of the army had been struck down, and many of the Highlanders had been taken prisoner. Old Alasdair MacIain and the other chiefs saw that this spring of 1690 would not give them their proper chance at a challenge to William's rule. Buchan mustered the clans to fight in several skirmishes, yes, and the forces of William's government harried the Highlands and the Isles, but all knew that the great battle, the momentous one, would be in Ireland, not so far to our west.

There, beside the River Boyne, our King James stood in early July with 25,000 soldiers, most of them Irish. William had brought his fleet from England, and had landed in the north of Ireland, where he enjoyed his greatest support, about two weeks before. From Belfast, he came south to the banks of the Boyne, just thirty miles from Dublin, commanding 36,000 men from his England, his Holland and his Lowlands of Scotland.

Early in the morning, William went about his attack, sending his loyal Dutchmen across the river. No Gael would have wished them well, but neither could any Gael have denied that the Dutchmen showed their strength. The Irish fired volley after volley at them as they pushed across the river on foot. Yet the Dutch returned fire even as they crossed, even as their feet sank, and then held their ground once the Irish cavalry came over them. With this foothold upon James' side of the river, more of William's forces were able to cross, and yet more, but only after hundreds of losses were they able to push back the Irish.

James had preserved much of his army, and thus could have repulsed William's men back across the river. Still, rather than rally his men for victory, he began to worry that an eventual escape route to Dublin might be imperilled by William's cavalry. Even as our Irish cousins were preparing to attack, James ordered them to retreat. The Irish had lost less than a tenth of their army, and they wished dearly to fight on, to defeat William, but James would not give them the chance.

Convinced, somehow, that his cause in Ireland was lost, he rode ahead of his retreating army, boarded a French vessel, and sailed away. He was in exile, once again, among our French allies. Many of his Irish supporters, enraged, left the army and returned to their homes, and a few days later, William and the English marched into Dublin.

When word of James' flight reached the Highlands and the Isles, our chiefs' hopes waned. Our people could expect little support from Ireland now, and though it was hoped that France would aid our cause, Alasdair MacIain and the other chiefs wondered whether Louis XIV would place his trust in a sovereign who had abandoned his men.

Still, James was our king, for loyalty cannot be disowned. If it could be, then it would hold no merit, it would have no meaning whatsoever. It would be nothing but a word.

Too, a French fleet had crushed the English navy off Beachy Head one day before the Battle of the Boyne, and thus a French invasion of England did not appear so improbable. With James and Louis returning to the north, the Highlanders might enjoy, at last, our deserved fight. This was not a time for lunging, but for caution, a time to wait for news of James' plans, France's intentions.

Yet, throughout the summer and autumn of 1690, William's government pressed into the Highlands. Archibald Campbell, Earl of Argyll, took his new regiment to the Isle of

Mull and burned all that he could of the MacLeans' lands. His servants took Castle Stalker from the Stewarts of Appin, our neighbours and allies. Every day, English ships passed among the waters off of the Isles. Hundreds of infantrymen from the 32-gun ship *Dartmouth* laid waste to the Isles of Gigha, Cara and Colonsay. They killed so many of the people of the Isle of Eigg. Mackay, the commander whom we had defeated at Killiecrankie the previous year, built a new fort just north of our glen, and it was garrisoned with 1,200 redcoats under Governor John Hill.

The Parliament in Edinburgh honoured it with the name of Fort William.

As the people of Glen Coe celebrated *Samhuinn* at the close of October, as the snows built upon *Bidean nam Bian*, James' court in Paris was rich with talk of the coming invasion. As the new year of 1691 began, as the sun came over *Sgorr nam Fiannaidh*, over *Sgorr na Cìche* and the stretching ridge of *Aonach Eagach*, as the taste of the salted cattle lost much of its novelty, there were yet more rumours from Paris of James' return.

For the next few months, Governor John Hill wrote his earnest letters to the chiefs, including Alasdair MacIain, urging them to submit to William. Again and yet again the chiefs refused. For all of the government's forts and regiments, our people remained loyal. John Hill, Archibald Campbell, and the rest of them could not conquer us.

In April, then, word reached the Highlands of Louis' victory over William at Mons, across the English Channel in Flanders. Louis' massive army threatened William more than ever before. With this, William and his advisors knew that they would need every last man they could summon to fight upon the Continent. It did not help them that many of their soldiers were yet in Ireland, for our cousins there had not surrendered when James ran away; they continued the fight, they kept to their hearts, despite the defeat beside the Boyne. Pacifying us in the north, for a time, would enable William's government to shift men and guns south to Flanders, perhaps even to France itself.

Thus, William's servant John Dalrymple began to entertain a certain strategy. Dalrymple, the very man who had gone to London to give the Scottish throne to William and Mary just two years before, the very man who had dreamed for long of binding England and Scotland together, was now of course the Secretary of State for Scotland. His strategy had been whispered before, but only now did the men in Edinburgh and London take it seriously: If William could not subdue the Highlanders with force, perhaps he could subdue us with money. While James remained away from us, dithering at Louis' château outside of Paris, perhaps English gold could buy a peace, for a short while.

Into this opening stepped a Campbell. It was not, however, Archibald Campbell, William's loyal Earl of Argyll, but his dear cousin John Campbell, the Earl of Breadalbane. He was the chief of the Campbells of Glen Orchy, who had gotten their lands through a most convenient marriage, centuries before. Besides being Archibald Campbell's cousin, he was married to Archibald's aunt Mary. Among the kindred and servants of the Campbells, he was second only to the Earl of

Argyll himself.

He was fifty-five years old or so in the spring of 1691, several years younger than our chief Alasdair MacIain, and he was pale, with thin lips, holding a grave expression nearly all of the time. Among the Gaels he was called *Iain Glas*, Grey John, for he rarely held to one view, or to one cause. Two years before, he had privately expressed his support to William, but had refused to provide him with troops. When called upon to fight for James, he had responded that, though he had dearly wished to join the clans, he had suffered a regrettable attack of gout, just then, that would keep him and all his men away. One who knew him well said that he was "cunning as a fox, wise as a serpent, slippery as an eel."

Now, with James in Paris, Grey John was publicly on the side of William, but kept in earnest correspondence with our chiefs, never firmly disavowing James. He was, as the chiefs knew, "Willie's man in Edinburgh and Jamie's in the Highlands."

In May, he went to London and dutifully presented his *Proposals Concerning the Highlanders* to William and Parliament. He claimed to know the hearts and peculiarities of each of the chiefs better than any other man; as a Highlander himself, he was best positioned to speak reason to them, and to be trusted. The Englishmen agreed, depositing £12,000 into his London bank account and sending him back north. Grey John sent messengers to each of the chiefs, requesting their presence at his castle of Achallader, twenty miles southeast of Glen Coe, across the moor of Rannoch.

To the castle, at the close of June, came our Alasdair Mac-

Iain, Angus MacDonnell of Glen Garry, Coll MacDonald of Keppoch, and many more of the chiefs, each with a retinue of men. Beside the great fire, over a hospitable meal with claret and whisky, John Campbell of Breadalbane told them of William's offer. Campbell took each chief aside, promising him a set sum, trying to persuade.

Only one of the chiefs was treated differently. When Campbell spoke to Alasdair MacIain, standing tall with his long, white hair, he insisted that any money owed to Alasdair be reduced, in order to compensate Campbell for the cattle and other livestock that the men of Glen Coe had taken from his lands two years before, in the wake of the Highlanders' victory at Killiecrankie and our defeat at Dunkeld.

Hearing this, Alasdair left, refusing to sign William's agreement. Our men had killed redcoats and lost many of our own, and yet here was a concern with the value of Campbell cows. Before leaving, Alasdair told his sons and his tacksmen: "I fear mischief from no man so much as the Earl of Breadalbane."

Even so, many of the chiefs agreed to the truce, after hours of negotiating. Once the names were signed, once the claret was finished, Grey John rode south to London and delivered a sheet of signatures promising that the Highlanders would not fight against William and his government for a whole of four months.

He did not, however, tell the entire story to the English. He told but half of it. For the chiefs had not simply agreed to lay down their arms in exchange for gold. No, they had agreed to the truce only because Campbell had made another arrangement with them at Achallader Castle, a spoken compact, one that William and his Parliament were forbidden to know.

They were forbidden to know of it because this spoken treaty preserved the chiefs' loyalty to our King James. Its terms were clear. If James decided to invade England or Scotland, or if he refused to approve the written truce, then the chiefs would be released from that truce. If William violated the written truce, however, Grey John of Breadalbane himself would have to muster 1,000 Campbells and join the chiefs to fight for the imminent restoration of James as king.

In the middle of August, perceiving the business at Achallader Castle as a harbinger, William deigned to offer the people of the Highlands and Isles a promise: If their chiefs would just swear an oath of allegiance to him by the first day of the new year, 1692, then they would be pardoned for their treason. Their chiefs would be forgiven for any crimes laid against them.

Quickly, Alasdair MacIain and the other chiefs asked two messengers to steal south toward Paris, hoping that the two of them might reach our King James and learn of his designs. The will of our king would dictate whether Highlanders would take William's oath quickly, or take it only with a strategic delay, or take it not at all. The two messengers, George Barclay and Duncan Menzies, slipped away from Scotland in late August, dodging William's troops and police all along their way, from Edinburgh down into England and then across the Channel. By the close of September, they were at the château of Saint-Germain-en-Laye, being greeted by James himself.

Yet no answer came from James during those last few days of September. Nor did one come in the month of October, nor, even, in November. Barclay and Menzies were requested to remain at James' court in exile, week upon week throughout the autumn, while ministers debated and James corresponded with the French.

As December of 1691 began, just one month from the deadline imposed by William, James still had not issued his decision. In our glen, and throughout the lands of the Gaels, many suspected that James had no stomach for the fight. John MacDonald, Alasdair MacIain's tacksman of Achtriachtan, obtained a letter of protection from the Governor of Fort William, John Hill, who hoped this gesture showed that Achtriachtan's chief would submit soon. Whispers and messages across Scotland, England, and France told of a new invasion from the south, while other whispers, other messages, told of chiefs who were about to give up on that weakling James.

In London, in the meanwhile, John Dalrymple was putting the plan into place. As Secretary of State for Scotland, he sat in elegant quarters of Kensington Palace, meeting Queen Mary regularly while William was at war on the Continent, exchanging letters with his loyal friends John Campbell of Breadalbane and Archibald Campbell, the Earl of Argyll.

The plan had been discussed for some time, of course. Grey John of Breadalbane knew it very well, as did his cousin Archibald. The Earl of Argyll's regiment would be the one.

Dalrymple was convinced, however, that Governor John Hill of Fort William was too accommodating to the Highlanders, and might disrupt the operation. Hill, after all, was the man who had granted a letter of protection to our John MacDonald of Achtriachtan, besides other Highland men.

Dalrymple decided to deal with Fort William's Deputy Governor, James Hamilton, instead. Like Dalrymple, Hamilton was a Lowlander, and he had fought hard against the Irish people and our James. In his letters to the south, Hamilton had written that he was eager to confront the Highlanders, eager to "put in execution such commands as shall come for reducing them to better manners."

Dalrymple, knowing the right man without yet being honoured by his acquaintance, sent Hamilton an introductory letter that read: "It may be shortly we may have use of your garrison, for the winter time is the only season in which we are sure the Highlanders cannot escape us, nor carry their wives, children and cattle into the mountains." Dalrymple did not tell very much more in this first letter. No, he decided to wait two days, so that Hamilton had two full nights of sleep before receiving the next message.

That message read: "The MacDonalds will fall into this net....Let me hear from you whether you think that this is the proper season to maul them in the long, cold nights."

Chapter 23

Uncle Angus

An envelope came in the mail, and it was from Virginia. From Kathy Vockery in Garrard County, Kentucky, I'd learned that my ancestor Angus McDonald might have lived in Amherst County, Virginia before migrating to Kentucky in the 1780s or 1790s. Then, online, I'd found the Amherst County Museum & Historical Society, emailing them to ask for help. And now here was this envelope.

The cover letter was written by hand, signed by Charles Hamble, Volunteer Researcher. Though most of the Amherst County records were held at the courthouse, the Museum & Historical Society had a large collection of books by genealogists who'd read through some of those records and had transcribed them. Charles had taken the time to look through all the books for me, and had enclosed copies of everything he'd found.

He hadn't been able to uncover a marriage record for my Angus in Amherst County, nor in any of the surrounding counties, and not a single will or probate record from the area mentioned Angus. But there were land records—an Angus McDonald or McDaniel bought and sold several tracts in Amherst County in the 18th century.

The first one was dated May 9, 1767, showing that Angus McDaniel had 99 acres of land surveyed along Brown Mountain Creek. Then, a year later, another 82 acres were surveyed for their owner Angus McDaniel along the north branches of the Pedlar River.

This went on for the next twenty years, several land purchases in the name of Angus McDaniel: On both sides of the north fork of the Buffalo River, and by Nicholson's Run, and at the head of the south branches of the Pedlar River, and soon I found that the land surveyed for Angus McDaniel in 1775 was recorded as the property of Angus McDonald in 1784.

Then there was this 1772 deed of trust between Angus McDaniel and the George Kippen Company, merchants of Glasgow, Scotland. Angus had mortgaged 156 acres to the merchants, and from the description of the land, I could tell that it was a tract he'd purchased just two years before. Why did Angus have to mortgage land that he'd just recently bought? Did this hint at a family connection to Glasgow?

And the more I looked, the more I could see that all these records, from 1767 into the 1790s, referred to the same man. On a map, Charles had highlighted the creeks and rivers that served to mark off the pieces of land belonging to an Angus McDaniel or Angus McDonald, and all the tracts were within two or three miles of one another, tucked away in the northwestern corner of the county. The 1767 purchase and the 1775 purchase, for instance, looked to be just a mile apart, and both were recorded as being adjacent to the land of William Taylor. Angus had decided to settle right next to the Blue Ridge Mountains, in the hills.

Charles had discovered one other thing from the land records: Some of Angus' parcels were near the lands of a George McDaniel and a John McDaniel. My ancestor Angus had sons named George and John, so were these two men related to Angus?

But all right, time to step back. I was getting ahead of myself. Because none of the land records proved that this Amherst County Angus was *my* Angus. Thousands of Scottish Highlanders emigrated to Virginia before the Revolutionary War, so the Angus McDonald/McDaniel who appeared in Amherst County, Virginia in 1767 might have been a different man entirely. I needed to find a piece of evidence clearly showing that Amherst County Angus was identical to the Angus McDonald who lived in Garrard County, Kentucky from the 1790s to 1828.

In this envelope from Charles, though, I found a clue. In 1794, Richard Ballinger and his wife Elizabeth sold land that had once been owned by Angus McDonald, and in connection with the sale, there was a Kentucky link: Justices of the Peace for Mercer County, Kentucky "quizzed Elizabeth Ballinger and Martha McDaniel apart from their husbands."

Now, I knew that part of Mercer County had been split off in 1797 to form Garrard County, where my ancestor Angus lived, and Internet posts said that some of my Angus' children had gotten married in Mercer County prior to that year. So, before 1797, my Angus probably lived in the part of

Mercer County that split off to become Garrard County— and here was a Martha McDaniel of Mercer County being "quizzed" in 1795, apart from her husband, regarding land that once belonged to Angus McDonald of Amherst County, Virginia.

If this Martha was the wife of my Angus in Kentucky in 1795, then he just had to be Amherst County Angus. And if Martha *was* his wife, then she very well could be my ancestor, too, the mother of my ancestor John, who was probably born in the 1780s.

To find out, I'd have to explore the Amherst County records, the ones that might not have made their way into the books on the Museum & Historical Society's shelves. I was thinking about boarding the train in New York and heading southwest, but when I looked at sites devoted to Virginia genealogy, I learned that a copy of every record, from every county courthouse, was available on microfilm at the Library of Virginia in Richmond, the capital.

Well, then. What if the names of my Angus' parents were right there, in one easily found document on microfilm? Why travel all that way, only to find out in a matter of minutes that the search would have to shift to someplace else entirely? Better to get a first read from someone else, and then figure out things from there. At the Library of Virginia site, I found a list of professional genealogists in the area, and after a quick email, James Ward agreed to take me on.

Several weeks later, James' findings arrived in a white folder. He summarized the Amherst County records in a few pages, and I scanned over the first page, and then the second, with all these paragraphs mentioning McDonalds and Mc-Daniels, until I saw: "11 April 1803—Angus McDaniel and his wife, Martha, of County of Garrard and State of Kentucky to Henry Camden…110 acres on the head branches of Pedlar and Richeson Creek on the lines of David Moore, James Frazier, Nicholson Run, William Taylor."

I went back to the land records that Charles Hamble had discovered. This 110 acres, sold by Angus and Martha McDaniel of Garrard County, Kentucky in 1803, was the same 110 acres that Angus McDaniel had bought in 1775, along Nicholson Run, adjacent to the land of William Taylor. And that 1775 Angus was the same Angus McDaniel/McDonald who appeared again and again in the Amherst County records from 1767 into the 1790s.

Now I knew it for certain: My ancestor Angus McDonald was in Amherst County, Virginia, right next to the Blue Ridge Mountains, by May of 1767, and his wife in the 1790s and early 1800s was a woman named Martha, who could be the mother of my ancestor John. Since Angus died in 1828, and first appeared in the records in 1767, it appeared that he was born in about 1740.

But how did Angus move to Amherst County to begin with, and who was Martha, and how did they end up as husband and wife? Where did they come from?

James hadn't uncovered a marriage record for Angus and Martha, and he hadn't found a will or probate record for either of them. This first round of searching, in fact, didn't lead to any records in Amherst County that revealed the parents or other relatives of Angus or Martha. But James had uncovered one new hint.

My Angus' neighbors, George and John McDaniel, were brothers, and George bought land from my Angus in 1780. George and John's father, George McDaniel, Sr., left a will in Amherst County in 1818, but it didn't include Angus in the list of George, Sr.'s children. That suggested Angus wasn't his son. Still, these records raised the possibility that George, Jr. and John were related to my Angus, perhaps as cousins. If they were, then following their family tree might lead me to mine.

If all I had to go on were these old documents, I probably would have come away suspecting that George and John were related to my Angus, at least on Angus' father's side, but I would have had no way of knowing for sure. But with DNA, I had a chance of figuring this out. Was there some patrilineal descendant of George, Jr. or John whose DNA signature could be compared to Uncle Chuck's?

Before stalking for any more cheek swabs, I went to Ysearch.org, a site that allows people to submit their DNA markers, no matter which company they'd submitted their DNA to. I searched through the McDaniels, and after a while, I found a man who was patrilineally descended from the brother of George McDaniel, Sr., of Amherst County— paternal uncle of George, Jr. and John. Assuming there hadn't been a non-paternity event, this man had the same DNA signature as the two McDaniel brothers who lived next to my ancestor Angus.

And looking through the DNA markers, there was no doubt: He had the signature of Somerled, the signature that

Penny and I had heard Bryan Sykes discuss on the Isle of Skye during our honeymoon. The fact that this man had the Mc-Daniel/McDonald name, along with the Somerled signature, meant that my Angus' neighbors George, Jr. and John were descended from the MacDonald chiefs. They had the same DNA signature as the chiefs of every branch of Clan Donald.

Except for Glencoe.

Since the Amherst County McDaniels didn't have the Glencoe DNA signature, they couldn't have been the paternal cousins of my Angus McDonald. George McDaniel, Jr. and his brother John McDaniel knew my Angus McDonald very well, and they lived next to him for years, but they came from a different family, at least on their father's side. These McDaniels might have been maternally related to my Angus, or they might have been his in-laws, but if I were going to discover Angus' father, with his Glencoe DNA, then I'd have to look elsewhere.

Which brings us to the mystery of Uncle Angus.

In that 1821 court record from Garrard County, Kentucky, my Angus said that his uncle Angus McDonald had served in the French & Indian War of 1756 to 1763, also known as the Seven Years War. As a reward for his service, Uncle Angus had been awarded land that had been "entered, surveyed and granted to John Savage and Company." Uncle Angus must have served alongside this John Savage, whoever he was.

I went to Google, typed "John Savage French and Indian War," and was taken to a site about the Savage Land Grant. In 1754, the site said, the Governor of Virginia promised land to any man who would join the Virginia militia for the coming fight against France. John Savage was a captain in the militia, and after the war ended, King George III granted more than 27,000 acres to Savage and fifty-nine other militiamen. The site listed them, one by one, and I quickly saw that name: Angus McDonald.

This had to be Uncle Angus. My ancestor Angus, writing in 1821 as an old man in Kentucky, had gotten it right about his uncle, about a land grant in Virginia roughly half a century before.

Maybe there were some records connected to the Savage Land Grant that would reveal who Uncle Angus was. The first place to look was right here, on this page, where I'd found these clues about John Savage and Uncle Angus. The page was on the KYOWVA Genealogical and Historical Society site, devoted to the counties where Kentucky, Ohio, and West Virginia meet. These were the counties—part of the furthest reaches of Virginia at the time—where King George's rewards had been placed.

I emailed the KYOWVA Society and got a response from the Society's librarian. Uncle Angus had been granted Lot #41, she wrote, right next to the tract allotted to John Savage himself. Uncle Angus' lot comprised 400 acres that lay in the middle of modern day Huntington, West Virginia. That's all she knew offhand, she wrote, but she'd be willing to look through the library's records and tell me what was known regarding Uncle Angus.

And just a few days later, she emailed again, telling what she'd learned.

Uncle Angus never lived on his 400 acres, but he never sold it, either. It passed to his daughter Anne, wife of Richard Holliday of Hampshire County, Virginia, and then, in 1809, Anne and Richard sold all 400 acres. Uncle Angus had given the land to Anne in his will, probated in 1778 in Frederick County, Virginia.

No, that couldn't be right. That had to be wrong. It just had to be. Because I'd already read about Colonel Angus Mc-Donald of Frederick County, Virginia, and there was no way that he could be my Uncle Angus.

Colonel Angus McDonald was a prominent man in Frederick County in the 1760s and 1770s, a confidant of George Washington and a well-regarded soldier—and a patrilineal descendant of the MacDonalds of Glengarry, not the Mac-Donalds of Glencoe. His gorget, an ornamental collar, was engraved with the Glengarry coat of arms. He even named his house and plantation Glengarry. According to his descendants, he fought with the Glengarry MacDonalds in the rebellion of 1745, but was forced to flee to Virginia in 1747 or so.

It wasn't just the Glengarry connection that made me suspect Colonel Angus and Uncle Angus were different people. In the 1821 Garrard County, Kentucky court record, my ancestor Angus wrote that he was Uncle Angus' "only heir resident in America," but Colonel Angus had several sons and daughters who lived into adulthood in the United States and were alive and well in 1821.

Besides, Virginia militia records showed that the Angus McDonald who served with John Savage and George Washington on the Virginia frontier—the one who was entitled to the 400 acres as part of the Savage Land Grant—was twenty-one years old when he enlisted in 1754, which meant he was born in 1732 or 1733. But Colonel Angus' descendants all said that he was born in about 1727, old enough to fight in Scotland in 1745 and 1746.

Somebody had to be wrong. The question was: Who?

I looked online for any Angus McDonalds or MacDonalds or McDaniels or McDonnells who might have served in the French and Indian War in America. Because maybe my Uncle Angus of Glencoe had been granted this land only to have it taken away by Colonel Angus of Glengarry, who might have innocently thought the land was his, or not.

The searching took me to several books, and to a few genealogists, but after months of looking and note-taking and waiting, I'd found no other Angus McDonald who could have rightfully claimed that 400 acres other than Colonel Angus. Every record suggested that the Col. Angus McDonald who lived in Frederick County in the 1760s and 1770s was identical to the Angus McDonald who fought with John Savage and George Washington in the French and Indian War, and who was entitled to Lot #41 of the Savage Land Grant.

Well, somebody had to be lying—either my ancestor Angus or Colonel Angus of Frederick County.

And as I was going through all these online records and old books, I discovered more and more McDonalds and McDaniels living in Virginia and Maryland in the second half of the 18th century. There were several Anguses, several Johns, an Allen or two, at least one Alexander. But none of them lived in Amherst County, as far as I could tell, so I had no way of knowing whether they were related to my Angus.

This one clue, though, this one Angus, might lead somewhere. Through a short entry on the Library of Virginia site, and with the help of genealogist Anne Taylor Brown, I learned of an Angus McDonald of Hampshire County, Virginia who emigrated to America from Scotland in 1766, the son of Archibald McDonald. My Angus first appeared in Amherst County in May 1767, so he very well could have emigrated just before then—what if he'd emigrated in 1766 along with these two other McDonalds?

I had trouble finding any online records about Angus of Hampshire County, Virginia or his father Archibald, except for one thing: This Angus married a woman named Anne Doyle in Allegany County, Maryland in 1798. Allegany County was in western Maryland, and sure enough, there were a few Internet references to McDonalds and McDaniels in that area. So I found Michael Hait, who said he'd look into some of the Maryland records at the state archives in Annapolis.

His findings came in an email, with PDFs attached. There were no wills or probate records for an Angus McDonald, he reported back, but an Angus McDonald bought several tracts of land in western Maryland in the 1760s and 1770s. Looking through the deeds and patents, I could tell, almost immediately, that this was Colonel Angus of Frederick County, Virginia. His wife Anne Thompson was from Maryland, not far from Frederick County, and Colonel Angus had bought many acres of land that had belonged to Anna's brothers.

Oh, well. This wasn't what I'd been hoping for, but just in case something here was interesting, I should go ahead and look through the PDFs.

Then I let out a little gasp in my mind.

One of the tracts that Colonel Angus bought was on the Potomac River, and it began at a spot "standing opposite a high peaked hill." Anna's brothers had named the land after their parents, but after purchasing it, Colonel Angus decided to give it a new name.

Glencoe.

My ancestor Angus McDonald swore, in a Kentucky court in 1821, that Uncle Angus had received a tract as part of the Savage Land Grant. And now I knew that Colonel Angus McDonald of Frederick County, Virginia not only received that particular tract, but named some of his land in Maryland after the very same glen where my Angus' ancestors lived.

Colonel Angus *was* Uncle Angus.

But how could this be, given that Colonel Angus' ancestors were known to be from Glengarry, rather than Glencoe? I could think of two scenarios that made sense.

Scenario One: Uncle Angus, a.k.a. Colonel Angus, was my Angus' maternal uncle, not his paternal uncle. Under this scenario, my Angus' mother was a Glengarry MacDonald:

Glengarry MacDonald

Glencoe MacDonald ─┬─ My Angus' Mother   Uncle Angus
                   │   (c.1733-1778)
         My ancestor Angus (c. 1740-1828)

Then there was Scenario Two: Uncle Angus, a.k.a. Colonel Angus, was the half-brother of my Angus' father. Under this scenario, my Angus' grandmother married a Glencoe MacDonald, but then married a Glengarry MacDonald:

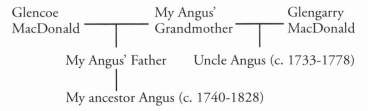

Glencoe   My Angus'   Glengarry
MacDonald ─┬─ Grandmother ─┬─ MacDonald

My Angus' Father   Uncle Angus (c. 1733-1778)

My ancestor Angus (c. 1740-1828)

I didn't know which scenario was true, but each one fit the facts. Each one explained how my ancestor Angus could have had an uncle who shared his surname, but who didn't share his patrilineal ancestry. Each one explained how Uncle Angus could have had a connection to Glencoe despite having a Glengarry MacDonald father.

If Scenario Two were right, then it was even possible that Uncle Angus had Glencoe ancestry himself—his mother might have been from Glencoe, and so he could have named the Maryland purchase after his maternal homeland, having named his Virginia plantation after his father's home.

Still, what about my ancestor Angus' 1821 claim that he was his uncle's "only heir resident in America?" Colonel Angus had several children and grandchildren who were alive in the U.S. in 1821, so I'd figured that he couldn't be Uncle Angus.

But now that I knew more about my ancestor Angus' history in Virginia, I didn't see any contradiction at all. Several sources agreed that Colonel Angus married Anne Thompson in 1766, and they stayed in Frederick County all along, and their first child wasn't born until May 9, 1767—the same day that my Angus' first plot of land was surveyed in Amherst County, about 130 miles to the south.

That meant my Angus wouldn't have known about the birth and survival of Colonel Angus' first child unless the two of them had stayed in touch after that. My Angus very well could have come to Amherst County before May of 1767, before Colonel Angus was even married. And I could easily see how an uncle and nephew living 130 miles apart, along a mountainous frontier in the 18th century, wouldn't exactly be exchanging daily updates.

Now I had two leads to go on, not just one. Two counties in Virginia, two stories, two sets of McDonalds. James Ward had only gotten a chance to take a first look through the Amherst County records regarding my ancestor Angus, so there were many more of those to uncover, and now the Frederick County records awaited, too.

I was headed south.

CHAPTER 24

FÀILTE

Cha cho-ionann teine lùchairt is teine teallaich.

The fires in a palace burn differently than a hearth.

At King Louis XIV's château near Paris, where our men still waited for our King James' decision, the firewood surely arrived each morning, and if it did not, that was only because enough had been stocked the night before. During the cold of November and December, 1691, James had day after day to warm himself, day after day to think and wait, knowing that more would come tomorrow. The people of Glen Coe had long conserved even the charred wood, even the wee pieces of peat, but for those few who might live on unclocked time, urgency has no bite.

Too, at Kensington Palace near London, the logs came whenever needed. William's ministers and lawyers could bide the time, trusting that news from the north would come soon enough. The Highland chiefs, after all, would have to swear the oath to William by the 1st of January, barely more than three weeks away.

Still, William's Secretary of State for Scotland, John Dalrymple, continued with his plans, his orchestration of letters. From Grey John Campbell, Earl of Breadalbane, he learned that the chiefs, even now, insisted upon waiting for approval from James before taking the oath to William. Dalrymple responded that "the madness of these people, and their ungratefulness to you, makes me plainly see there is no reckoning on them; but *delenda est Carthago*...."

That phrase, from every good Englishman's second language, meant "Carthage must be destroyed." The Romans had repeated those words for decades until they succeeded in burning the whole of Carthage to the ground, selling all of its people into slavery. Every victory in Ireland and Scotland over the previous decades, and every new garrison in the lands of the Gaels, had demonstrated to the English and their Lowland servants that they might yet become the new Rome, expanding rightfully, inevitably, in each direction. Over the sea, even.

So it was that on the 15th of December, William's soldiers were given their orders to begin moving north and west. Seven companies of James Leslie's regiment marched toward Inverness, joined by six companies from John Buchan's regiment. Robert Lumsden's company, and George Murray's, as well, were added to Governor John Hill's forces at Fort William. The 800 redcoats belonging to the regiment of Archibald Campbell, Earl of Argyll, were told that they, too, would soon be sent to Fort William.

Yet Dalrymple did not know that, just a few days before, on the 12th of December, our King James had finally made his decision: He would lead no invasion, and the chiefs were free to swear the oath to William.

Our messenger, Duncan Menzies, left the château in haste, but though he rushed north, taking the swiftest coaches and ships and hardly sleeping, he was unable to reach Edinburgh until the 21st. Travelling north, he arrived at his home the next day, still miles from the Highlands, and collapsed of exhaustion. Messengers had to be found, and they did not leave Menzies' home until Christmas Eve. From there, they rode as quickly as possible through the ice and snow, but most of the chiefs did not learn of James' decision until after Christmas, just a few days before the deadline.

Alasdair MacIain of Glen Coe was among the last of the chiefs to receive the news, and he immediately set out for Fort William. Like the rest of our people, Alasdair had hoped that James would return and fight, but our king was alive, all the same, with a healthy heir and powerful allies in Scotland, France and elsewhere. The winds very well could shift soon. Signing William's piece of paper meant a mere pause.

On the 31st of December, white-haired Alasdair was escorted into Governor Hill's room at Fort William, and standing tall in his plaid above every other man, he asked to give the oath. Hill was happy to see that Alasdair had come before the deadline, but there was nothing that he could do: He was a military official, and William's law required, instead, that the submission be given before a sheriff or a sheriff's deputy.

Alasdair would have to travel to the Campbell stronghold of Inveraray, a sixty-mile journey to the south, and profess his loyalty to King William in front of the sheriff, Sir Colin Campbell.

With no true chance at meeting the deadline, Alasdair nonetheless left for Inveraray, hoping that he would somehow be permitted to take the oath. The shortest route would take him through the mountains, but the driving snow prevented it, and thus Alasdair had to go the longer way, along the coast, before finally arriving at Inveraray on the 2nd of January.

Yet Alasdair would have to wait, for Colin Campbell was away with his family, celebrating Hogmanay. The New Year, as you call it. He alone could accept the oath on William's behalf, and so for three days, our chief remained in a small inn, never venturing outside, never giving his name, surrounded by soldiers and Campbells.

Only on the 5th did Colin Campbell return, and Alasdair went to him immediately and handed him a letter written by Governor Hill. It explained that Alasdair had "slipped some days, out of ignorance," and implored Campbell to accept MacIain's oath, for "it is good to bring in a lost sheep at any time." Campbell read the letter, and considered it for a time. William's edict did not provide any exceptions to the deadline, to be sure. Still, Campbell was regarded as a fair man, and though he hated the MacDonalds, Hill's letter made plain that the chief of Glen Coe had wholly intended to offer his submission in time.

Campbell allowed MacIain to take the oath.

At that, Alasdair returned to our glen, where the news was soon known by all. At Inverrigan and Dalness, at Achtriachtan and Laroch, at Invercoe beside Alasdair's house, a comfort came over our people for the first time in months. Though our chief had taken the oath, others of the MacDonalds had not, and some worried that harm might come to our cousins of Glen Garry, of Clan Ranald and of the Isle of Skye. The MacLeans, too, had withheld their submission.

It was scarcely a few days later, on the evening of the 12th, that someone interrupted John Dalrymple from his letter-writing at Kensington Palace. His servant informed him that Archibald Campbell, Earl of Argyll, had come with a message. Campbell was welcomed in, and told Dalrymple of the events of the north. Campbell owned a great house in London, as did his cousin John Campbell of Breadalbane, and over the previous days, the two of them had met with Dalrymple about what was to be done.

Dalrymple thanked Campbell, bade him good-bye, and returned to his letter, addressed to King William's Commander-in-Chief for Scotland, Thomas Livingstone. Dalrymple wrote: "Just now my Lord Argyll tells me that Glen Coe has not taken the oath, at which I rejoice. It's a great work of charity, to be exact, in rooting out that damnable sept, the worst in all the Highlands."

Though other clans had been late, we were the smallest one, and it took only a few days for papers to be drawn up. In London on the 16th of January, 1692, the document was placed before His Majesty William III, King of England, Scotland, and Ireland. William read it all, and was satisfied. He dipped his quill into the ink and signed. The final sentence read: "If MacIain of Glen Coe and that tribe can be well separated from the rest, it will be a proper vindication of the public justice to extirpate that sept of thieves."

King William's order was sent to Governor Hill at Fort

William, and the Commander-in-Chief, Thomas Living-stone, soon wrote to James Hamilton, the Deputy Governor there: "So, Sir, here is a fair occasion for you to show that your garrison serves for some use....I desire that you would begin with Glen Coe and spare nothing which belongs to him, but do not trouble the Government with prisoners."

On the 1st of February, 120 soldiers from the regiment of Archibald Campbell, Earl of Argyll, marched toward Glen Coe. One of our men saw them coming and ran ahead to Alasdair MacIain, who quickly ordered his people to hide our weapons up toward the mountains, away from our houses. Alasdair had given the oath, and thus we had little to fear, but that would not prevent the government from confiscating our people's arms, if they could be found.

Alasdair's son John went forward with several men to meet the soldiers, and beside Loch Leven, John asked what brought them to Glen Coe. Lieutenant John Lindsay, standing at the front, answered that they had come in peace. The garrison at Fort William was full, he said, and so it was necessary that the soldiers find food and lodging nearby for a short time.

Lieutenant Lindsay handed John the orders from his su-perior officer, which, indeed, authorised the quartering of the troops. John saw that the orders had been signed by Governor Hill, the very man whose letter had enabled Alasdair MacIain to take the oath despite being late, the very man whose signed letter of protection was still in the possession of our tacksman, John MacDonald of Achtriachtan.

Now the captain of the company stepped forward. His name was Robert Campbell, and he was a cousin of the Earl of Argyll and of Grey John Campbell of Breadalbane. He was sixty years old, with red-blonde hair, and tall. He loved to drink, to laugh and gamble, to tell stories. Among the first words he uttered to John MacIain were: "How is my nephew?"

For Robert Campbell was our own kin.

His niece Sarah was married to Alasdair Og, son of Alasdair MacIain and brother of John. Campbell shook John's hand and promised that Lieutenant Lindsay's words were true: The soldiers needed quartering only because of the crowding at Fort William, and it was needed for just a few days, before the regiment would be called to Glen Garry to police the rebels there. Campbell was of Glen Lyon, a Gael, who spoke our tongue and lived in our way. He knew very well our law of hospitality.

John looked at Campbell, and welcomed him and his soldiers into our glen.

Sergeant Robert Barber was welcomed into the home of Angus MacDonald, Achtriachtan's younger brother, and his men were brought into the houses thereabouts, upon the field of Achnacon. Campbell himself was invited to the home of our chief, Alasdair MacIain, but he chose instead to stay in the stone house of our tacksman of Inverrigan, in the woods. All along the glen, doors were opened, and soldiers ducked their heads to come in.

The older children would have to sleep in the corners, but they would be able to bear it. We would keep the fires burning for them, and the heat would settle over them. We would drape our plaids over them. Yes, they would have to bear it for now, but only for the next few days.

Too, we had enough heather to bring out, and we could stretch it upon the ground so that each soldier would have a place to sleep. We had water from the River Coe and from the mountains, and so they would not be thirsty.

At dinner that first night, we asked them to our fires, and our whisky was brought to them. They thanked us, and some of the Gaels among them gave us a toast. Soon the salted meat was hung above the fire until cooked well. We offered it to them, and they took it kindly. They were hungry from their march, it was plain to see.

Long after the meat was served, after the last one of them declined the last drink, we went to bed. In nearly every house, the last of us to retire needed to search for a space to lie down, laughing quietly, hoping not to stumble, for the soldiers were everywhere about the floor, their shoulders and heads and ankles. Aye, some of them snored.

So it was, not only that first night, but for the nights afterward. With each evening, with each new serving of beef and lamb, with each new round of whisky, all began to speak a bit more openly, a bit more plainly. The first jokes were made about Jamie and Willie, and the first guarded opinions were aired. So many of the soldiers were Gaels, who soon began telling some of the old tales.

We had our stories to tell, as well, and our bards recited the poems in our tongue while the Lowlanders and the Englishmen among them were given whispered summaries. When the first of the songs began, we knew we had made them comfortable, and every night after that, glances were met with smiles.

From then on, we treated them to dancing after all of us had finished dinner. Our bagpipes played the old songs. When the pipers performed the *Ceòl Mór*, the Great Music, with its traversals and intricacies, the soldiers listened silently.

We had the days with them, too, the mornings and afternoons after the fireside singing and drinking. The soldiers did drills for some of the time, but during most of the day, they were among us. We invited them to play shinty with us, and I should think the best men won. We had contests at archery, and, yes, some wagering. Now and then, some of the soldiers watched our women and children spin wool and make butter.

Captain Robert Campbell, like the rest of them, came into a routine soon enough. Upon rising from his heather bed at Inverrigan and taking a bit of breakfast, he would go to visit his niece Sarah and his nephew Alasdair Og, Alasdair MacIain's son. Sarah and Alasdair Og would welcome him into their house and give him a dram of whisky for the morning cold, and they would enjoy one another's company for a time. The days were for the soldiers' drilling, but each night, he would have dinner with Alasdair MacIain's sons, playing cards and backgammon beside the hearth as the whisky was passed about.

Campbell, then, was sitting with Alasdair Og and his older brother John on the evening of February 12th, after nearly two weeks with us. Dinner had been finished, and Campbell had rightly thanked the two MacIains for it. The three of them were playing cards and drinking whisky when they heard a knock upon the door. It was a messenger, carrying a letter from Campbell's superior officer.

Campbell opened it and read: "You are hereby ordered to fall upon the rebels, the MacDonalds of Glen Coe, and to put all to the sword under seventy."

Chapter 25

Alias Capias

Hoping to discover the parents of my ancestor Angus Mc-Donald in Virginia, I boarded a train in New York. We left in mid-morning, and before long I saw the Philadelphia skyline, and then the row houses of Baltimore. By lunch time, the Capitol Building was on the horizon, followed by the Washington Monument as we crossed the Potomac River. Soon we were out of the suburbs of northern Virginia, and the traffic thinned on the roads around us, and by late afternoon I was at my hotel in downtown Richmond.

The next morning, I walked a few blocks down the street to the Library of Virginia and finished my coffee on the marble steps outside. Up another flight of stairs, I came to a big room, two stories high, with tall windows letting in the sun.

It must have been obvious that I had no idea what I was doing, because a librarian approached me and offered to show me around. This room stored all the microfilm records and the reference books, she said, while that room on the other side of the stairs, the one I'd apparently passed by, stored all the county-specific texts. Now, right here was the desk where

I could find archivists who might point me the right way, and here were the computers that were equipped for microfilm viewing, and over there, stored in row after row of white file cabinets, were the microfilm rolls, mostly organized by county.

"All right, thank you very much," I said.

Right then, I didn't know that county clerks in 18th century Virginia often didn't take the time to compile useful things like indexes. So if you wanted to know what was contained in 700 pages of handwritten court records, you just might have to read through *700 pages of handwritten court records.*

Right then, walking toward the computers, I didn't know that the fish and chips at the Penny Lane Pub on Franklin Street were pretty good, and the chicken fingers weren't bad. Turkey sandwich at the Wall Street Deli? Not too shabby. The burritos at Cafe Olé were great for lunch, but the place was closed for dinner. Nice beer selection at the Capital Ale House, decent burgers.

Right then, signing in at the desk and getting set up at the computer, I actually believed I'd be here in downtown Richmond for just a day or two.

I went to the cabinets and found the A's: Alleghany, Amelia, Amherst. The roll fit into the microfilm reader that was attached to the computer, and in a few seconds I was scrolling through the 1766 court records of Amherst County, Virginia, from one yellowed page to the next, like it was an online photo album.

Reading through these court entries and deed books and wills, hour after hour, I found references to my Angus, but none of them revealed much about his origins or his family. I knew about each time he sued someone, each time he was sued himself, and the surveys detailed the location and dimensions of every piece of land he owned, but there were no clues about his parents, his siblings, his children.

Still, maybe I'd find some hints in records from nearby counties. My Angus lived just across the border from Augusta County, on the other side of the Blue Ridge Mountains, so I decided to look there. Searching through the Augusta County land records, I found a February 1786 deed involving my Angus—and his wife Martha. This was the same Martha who was mentioned as Angus' wife in 1795, and then again in 1803.

Now, based on censuses, Kentucky marriage records and information from distant cousins, it was clear that my Angus' 1826 will listed his children in order of birth, from the oldest to the youngest, and my ancestor John was last. Nancy, the one listed right before John, was born between 1782 and 1784, so John was probably born in the mid-1780s. His older sister Martha's marriage record listed her mother's name, and though it appeared to read "Patsy" (a nickname for Martha), there was a slight chance it read "Betsy" (a nickname for Elizabeth).

But now that I knew my Angus was married to Martha in early 1786, I had no doubt that the marriage record really did read "Patsy," and I never should have doubted my eyes anyway, and so Martha had to be the mother of those last few children listed in Angus' will, including my ancestor John. She was probably the mother of all of them, which was why

Angus referred to them, together, as "my first children." I had a new ancestor, and I added her name to the upper-right corner of my family tree:

Angus McDonald (c. 1740-1828), m. Martha
|
John McDonald (c. 1785-1828), m. Elizabeth Downing
|
Hiram McDonald (1806-1882), m. Nancy Buchanan
|
William Duncan McDonald (1855-1935), m. Georgianna Wilson
|
Will McDonald (1875-1964), m. Linnie Hagan
|
Lee McDonald (my great-grandpa), m. Mary Bridgewater
|
Betty McDonald (my grandma), m. Don McCord

I'd discovered Martha, but couldn't find any other Augusta County records involving her or her husband Angus, and the McDonalds and McDaniels in that county didn't seem to have a connection to my family. I looked all over Virginia for a marriage record, but there wasn't one. From what I could tell, the two of them had just shown up in 1767 in Amherst County, already married, living apart from any relatives.

But how did they get there, and where did they come from?

I picked up my notebook, walked to the help desk, and asked for help. The archivist, a middle-aged man wearing a tie, listened as I told him that I'd gone through all these records, and didn't know how my two ancestors came to this particular tract of land tucked under the Blue Ridge Mountains.

Their land was in western Virginia, and so I imagined that they first lived in eastern Virginia and migrated westward.

"Well, now," he said, "that *is* possible, but there's a much greater likelihood that they came from somewhere north, in fact." In the 1750s and 1760s, most people who migrated to Amherst County and the other western counties along the Blue Ridge Mountains came from northern Virginia, western Maryland, and Pennsylvania. The bulk of the migration wasn't from east to west, but from north to south, through the Shenandoah Valley, along the frontier.

As he said that, I saw the connection. My ancestor had an uncle, I told him, who lived in northern Virginia, in Frederick County, and who owned land in western Maryland. Winchester, the town where my ancestor's uncle lived, was a hub for people and goods traveling up and down the Shenandoah Valley and east to the Potomac River and the ocean. Perhaps my ancestor was part of the migration south through the valley, going to Amherst County from Frederick County.

"That very well could be, but of course you'd have to look into that," he said. "I can't give you an answer to that. But what was the name of your ancestor?"

"Angus McDonald."

"And what was the name of your ancestor's uncle?"

"Angus McDonald."

He grinned. "I see. So you'll want to keep in mind that those Scottish families were very tight." They usually emigrated together, and even if they emigrated separately, they often ended up living together once they were here in America.

It was quiet for a moment. I was writing all this down as

quickly as I could. He gave me another moment, and then said: "Now, let me just ask you one question, and you might not know the answer yet, but then you might. This Angus McDonald, the uncle—did he have any *mercantile* connections, by any chance?"

Actually, yes, he did. According to family tradition, I said, Uncle Angus was involved in a shipping and trading business in the port town of Falmouth, in northern Virginia, before joining the military in 1754.

He nodded, like he'd been expecting to hear me say just that. In the thirty years or so before the Revolutionary War, merchants from Glasgow dominated the economy of northern Virginia, buying tobacco from farmers in exchange for all sorts of goods. The heads of these Glasgow firms grew so wealthy that they came to be known as the Tobacco Lords, and they formed tight networks, often cementing alliances through marriage, employing family members and in-laws. It was common for young, Scottish men with Glasgow connections to come to the ports and towns of northern Virginia and work in the trading business.

Frederick County, here I come.

I headed toward the file cabinets, looked for the F's—Fluvanna, Franklin, Frederick—and brought back some rolls of microfilm to the computer. Threaded the first roll into the uptake reel, inched forward to the first page. And a whole new tale opened up.

Here was an Alexander McDonald, Sr., who was in Frederick County by 1752, a decade before Uncle Angus' first appearance in the county. From the court and chancery records, it looked like he was a merchant. Did Uncle Angus come to Frederick County because of this Alexander? Were they brothers, or maybe cousins?

Here, too, was an Alexander McDonald, Jr., and he was a schoolmaster. At first, I thought he had to be the son of Alexander, Sr., but then an archivist told me that in Virginia at the time, the words "Jr." and "Sr." were used to differentiate between two men of different ages living in the same area, whether or not they were father and son. So Alexander, Sr. certainly could be the father of Alexander, Jr., but it wasn't certain.

One thing *was* certain—Alexander McDonald, Jr. sued Alexander McDonald, Sr. in 1764. The suit was dismissed because Alexander, Jr. had recently moved out of the county, but the caption in this court entry at least said what the suit was about: Trespass, Assault, and Battery. On a completely unrelated note, Alexander, Sr.'s wife was brought into court in 1760 for "retailing liquors…without a license."

A John McDonald was here in Frederick County, as well, and in 1765, he sued Angus McDonald for trespass, assault, and battery, but he and Angus settled out of court. Here, then, was an Allen McDonald, making his first Frederick County appearance in 1771 as a defendant who'd been charged with—you guessed it—trespass, assault, and battery. John and Allen were the names that my Angus gave to his sons; maybe these men were my Angus' brothers or cousins. Maybe the McDonalds punched each other because they knew each other.

Even before coming to Richmond, I'd learned a lot about

John McDonald of Frederick County, and now, seeing these records, I suspected I might be on to something. John was a doctor, a close friend of Uncle Angus, and he and Uncle Angus served together as Justices of the Peace. In his will, Uncle Angus appointed this Dr. John McDonald to be his executor, the guardian of his children, and he gave Dr. John his sword, his sash, and his gorget engraved with the Glengarry coat of arms.

Through Clan Donald histories and online research, I'd discovered that Dr. John was the son of Archibald MacDonald, the tacksman of Achnancoichean, from the MacDonalds of Keppoch. Dr. John's sister was married to the Keppoch chief, and his great-great-grandfather Angus had been killed while fighting alongside the Glencoe chief against the Campbells in 1646. Here was the son of a MacDonald tacksman, who had a Glencoe connection and a close bond to Uncle Angus.

Now, according to family tradition, Uncle Angus may have been a descendant of the Glengarry chiefs on his father's side, and so he may have come from one of the Glengarry tacksmen's families. And my uncle Chuck's DNA matches suggested that my ancestor Angus might have been descended from one of the *Glencoe* tacksmen—Uncle Chuck was a closer match with Lachie (probable descendant of the 17th century Achtriachtan tacksmen) than he was with Colin (descendant of the 17th century Glencoe chiefs).

I remembered that many of the Highland emigrants to America before the Revolutionary War were the children or grandchildren of tacksmen, so were Uncle Angus, Dr. John, and my ancestor Angus among them?

All this history, and the names of these Frederick County McDonalds, were on my mind as I picked Reel #72 out of the file cabinet and threaded it onto the microfilm reader. I scrolled forward to the title page: Order Book 14, 1767-1770. These were the court records, indexed by the plaintiff's surname, and I'd already gone through the index and found a few McDonald plaintiffs, and had read their cases.

This time, though, I had the time to look for cases in which McDonalds weren't the ones suing, but the ones being sued. That meant reading through the list of plaintiffs, from A to Z, and seeing whether any McDonalds were listed as defendants. I started with the A's, didn't find anything, went to the B's, didn't find anything. Then I got to the C's and said to myself: All right, funny, don't think too much of it, let's see.

The case was called Campbell v. McDonald. Page 81.

I fast-forwarded to page 81 and saw: "Thomas Campbell v. John McDonald, Angus McDonald, and John McDonald, Jr." The date was August 7, 1767, and the caption read "In Debt." Campbell was claiming that the three McDonalds had borrowed money from him and hadn't paid him back. Nothing more was written about the lawsuit, but the next time the suit came before the court, it was May 7, 1768—exactly nine months later. There, on page 276, the court entry read:

"The Defendant John McDonald, Sr. being dead, this suit as to him is ordered to abate. The Defendant John McDonald, Jr. being no inhabitant of this colony, this suit as to him is discontinued. And the Defendant Angus McDonald not being arrested, on the motion of the Plaintiff by his attorney

244

an Alias Capias is ordered against him...."

Neither of these two Johns could be Uncle Angus' friend, Dr. John McDonald. This John McDonald, Sr. was dead by May 1768, while Dr. John lived until 1787. And this John McDonald, Jr., according to the court, left Virginia before May 1768, while the records showed that Dr. John lived in Frederick County in 1768, and was there for the rest of his life.

So, besides Dr. John, there were two John McDonalds in Frederick County before May 1768, and even though the words "Sr." and "Jr." didn't necessarily mean they were father and son, I suspected they were: They'd borrowed money together, which suggested a close relationship.

Now, what about this Angus McDonald, the one who was sued for the same debt? He was required to be in court that day, but hadn't shown up, and so an "alias capias" was issued against him. I Googled the phrase and learned that an alias capias was effectively an arrest warrant, compelling the sheriff to bring a defendant into court.

I was just wondering, and so I scrolled back a few pages to the first court entries for that date, and there I found it: "At a Court Continued and Held for Frederick County, May 7th, 1768. Present: Jacob Hite, Isaac Hite, Thomas Speake and Angus McDonald, Gent. Justices." Uncle Angus wasn't just sitting in the courtroom on May 7, 1768; he was one of the Gentlemen Justices hearing the case and issuing the arrest warrant.

The Angus McDonald who was sued by Thomas Campbell *couldn't be Uncle Angus.*

And after all these days of microfilm reading, all these genealogists' reports, all these days of online research and note-taking, I knew of only one Angus McDonald besides Uncle Angus who had a link to Frederick County. My ancestor Angus.

The scenario made perfect sense: My Angus lived in Frederick County with his family, became indebted to Campbell there, moved to Amherst County in 1767, and then was unable to be arrested in Frederick in 1768 because he no longer lived there. Unlike John McDonald, Jr., who was dismissed from the lawsuit because he'd left Virginia entirely by May 1768, Angus was issued an arrest warrant because he still lived in Virginia.

If I was right about this, and the Angus who was sued by Thomas Campbell was the same man as my Angus, then I was probably looking at a new ancestor. Because John McDonald, Sr. seemed to be the father of the other two men—John, Jr. and Angus—who were named in Campbell's lawsuit.

That took me back to a passage I'd uncovered in a book called *The Troublesome MacDonalds*. Written by Angus Henry McDonald, descendant of my ancestor Angus, the book didn't say much about my Angus' origins in Scotland, but it revealed a family story: The author's father, born in 1851, often "talked about our ancestors, about John or Andreas McDonald, who came over from the Highlands before the American Revolution. He must have meant Aeneas or Angus."

John *or* Angus McDonald. Why was the author's father unsure? Maybe because Angus' father was named John, and they immigrated together? I could see how, over a few generations, the family story could shift shape, but retain the right names.

Looking for more McDonald defendants in Frederick County, I went back to the earlier records, the ones from the 1740s and 1750s. Here, in 1750, was a case that read: "On the complaint of William Cochran against his servant Angers McDonnald for striking him…it is thereupon ordered by the court that the said Angers serve his said master one whole year after his time by Indenture, Custom or·Order of Court be expired for the same." This indentured servant Angus McDonald had punched his master, and he would have to serve an extra year for it.

The court date? February 13th.

The library was about to close, and this Richmond trip was done. Back in New York, over the next few weeks, I looked everywhere online for some clues about my Angus, about the John McDonald I suspected was his father, but couldn't find that proof I was looking for.

Then a reference at Ancestry.com took me to a University of Virginia site called *The Papers of George Washington*. Letters to and from Washington were reprinted here as images, and one of those letters was from a man named Daniel Campbell, in Falmouth. On June 28, 1754, Campbell wrote to Washington: "I sincerely thank you for the countenance you showed Angus McDonald on my account. I have been lately surprised with a story that he was shot for striking one of his officers, which I hope is false. If not, I pity his fate, and rather wish he had died as a soldier in the field of battle. If he is alive, please desire him to write me under your cover."

This Angus McDonald was definitely Uncle Angus—he was the only Angus McDonald serving under Washington in 1754. Daniel Campbell of Falmouth, Virginia had somehow taken Uncle Angus under his wing, connecting him to the rising star Washington. In this letter, Campbell almost wrote like a mentor.

I looked, and found that Daniel Campbell was a prominent Glasgow merchant and a cousin of the Campbell chiefs, the Earls and Dukes of Argyll. His partner Alexander Campbell was a cousin, as well. In the 1740s, 1750s and 1760s, Alexander and Daniel Campbell ran their trading business out of Falmouth and Fredericksburgh, two towns across the river from one another in northern Virginia.

Now I *really* wanted to go back to Richmond.

And once I was there, searching through the microfilm rolls and the books, I found out that Alexander and Daniel Campbell had loaned money to William Cochran of Frederick County—the same man who sued his young servant Angus McDonald on February 13, 1750. Record after record showed the trading links between Frederick County and the port towns of Falmouth and Fredericksburgh to the east.

It took a few more days of looking, though, before I found this record from Spotsylvania County, whose county seat was Fredericksburgh. On August 2, 1748, the court reported: "Angus McDonnald, a Servant belonging to Alexander and Daniel Campbell, was this day adjudged to be fourteen years of age towards payment of levies." They brought Uncle Angus into court to prove that he was under sixteen, so that they wouldn't have to pay any taxes on him.

Maybe I wouldn't discover anything more about the family of my ancestors Angus and Martha, and maybe I'd never know for certain that John McDonald was the father of my Angus. But now I knew how my Angus came to America. He was following his uncle, who had come to Virginia as a boy, the indentured servant of the Duke of Argyll's cousins.

Chapter 26

Beannachd
Leibh

B' e Donnchadh MacFhraing a' chiad dhiubh.

The first one was Duncan Rankin.

He was beside the River Coe in the early morning, before 5:00. Everyone else in the glen was yet asleep. A blizzard had arisen overnight, so that Duncan scarcely could see, and the wind froze against his skin, biting.

In the distance, he thought he could see the colour of red against the white of the driving snow. He waited a few moments, squinted his eyes again, and soon could see that a few redcoats were walking toward him.

They stabbed him in the chest with their bayonets. His body washed away down the river and into the loch.

Nearby, in a warm house, Robert Campbell and his lieutenants rose from their beds of heather. As our tacksman of Inverrigan awoke, Campbell's men grabbed him, and then grabbed his wife and children. The soldiers tied rope around all of their hands and feet, so that they could not move. The soldiers tied strips of cloth about their mouths, so that they could not scream. Then Campbell's men began to prepare their weapons. The children cried quietly.

Close by was the house of John, the elder son of Alasdair MacIain, and he awoke when he heard soldiers walking outside. He wrapped his plaid about him and walked to Inverrigan's house, knowing that Campbell was staying there. Through a window, Campbell saw him approaching, and quickly stepped outside so that he could meet John in front of the house.

John suspected the truth, and so Campbell made certain to greet him with warmth. Campbell said, "We at last have received our orders to proceed to Glen Garry, just as planned." Sensing that this was not enough, he looked at John and added, "Really, do you think that I would move against Glen Coe without warning my own niece and nephew, your brother?" Campbell's words rang true, for no Gael could murder his own kin. John turned and went back to his house.

Several minutes later, Campbell's watch struck 5:00, the hour that had been specified in his orders. Campbell nodded. The father, the mother, and their children were dragged outside and lined up. The soldiers shot them, and then ran their bayonets into them. The soldiers threw their bodies on a pile of animal dung.

A twelve-year-old boy living nearby was able to run over and approach Campbell without being harmed. He threw himself at Campbell's feet and begged for mercy. He said, "Please, sir, I will go anywhere with you if only you will spare me." The soldiers shot the boy as he lay on the ground.

Throughout the glen now, the soldiers were firing their muskets and stabbing their bayonets into our people. A few hundred yards away from Inverrigan, they pushed old Archibald MacDonald to the ground. They turned their muskets around and clubbed him. But they didn't kill him right then. Instead, they watched him crawl into a nearby house, and then they set fire to it.

Coming to another house, they listened. Fourteen people were inside, and parents were holding the mouths of their young children to keep them from making any noise. Yet someone made a sound. The soldiers blocked off the door and set fire to the thatched roof. The people inside tried to leave, pounding on the door and screaming to be let out. The soldiers watched the house burn down with everyone inside.

They killed a child, and all that would ever be found of her was her hand, lying in the snow. They saw an old man limping from a burning house and shot him down. They aimed their fire at the backs of people who were fleeing into the mountains.

At Achnacon, where a group of them under the command of Sergeant Robert Barber had been staying, Angus MacDonald was sitting at home with his wife and children and his older brother John, the tacksman of Achtriachtan. Soldiers came and stuck their rifles into the open windows. They fired. They ran into the house to find that they had killed everyone except Angus.

Before they could bayonet him, Angus said to them, "If you are going to kill me, please do it outside of my home." Sergeant Barber sneered and said, "Since I have eaten your meat, yes, I will do you the favour."

The soldiers brought Angus out and let him stand in front

of his house. They walked away for a distance, turned, and rushed toward him with their bayonets. But at the last moment, he threw his plaid over their heads and escaped toward *Sgorr nam Fiannaidh*. The soldiers grabbed his brother John's body and dragged it outside. They smeared animal dung on it.

Down the river, soldiers knocked on the door of Alasdair MacIain, and a servant answered. They told the servant that they now had to leave for Glen Garry, but had come to thank Alasdair for the hospitality he had shown them. The servant asked them to remain at the door, and he walked upstairs to the bedroom, where Alasdair and Lady Glen Coe were asleep. He woke them and passed on the message. Both of them rose from bed, and Alasdair asked that a dram of whisky be prepared for each of the soldiers, so that they could be shown on their way.

At that moment, the soldiers rushed up the stairs and into the bedroom. Alasdair stood in front of them, in his bed clothes. They shot him in the head, and then again in the back as he turned away. They stepped over his body to get to Lady Glen Coe. They stripped off her night gown. They grabbed her.

As she stood naked before them, they seized her hands. They forced her fingers into their mouths, and with their tongues and teeth, they pulled off each ring. They forced her down the stairs and out into the blizzard, where her heart soon stopped.

Nearby, her son John and his wife Eiblin handed their baby boy Alexander to a nurse, who wrapped the child in her plaid and ran into the darkness. John helped to guide the survivors as they went toward the mountain passes in the snow and wind, but the way to the nearest hearth was long. Many of those who were shivering and numb became pale after a short while. As they continued to walk, they became confused, stopping, unwilling to go farther. Then their skin became blue, and they began to speak of such odd things. Soon they could not talk or weep. They remained on the ground, and the strong ones tried to carry them, but the breath was gone.

Just after the survivors arrived into Appin, into Glen Creran and elsewhere, word spread throughout the Highlands and the Isles of what had happened. Before the 13th of February, many chiefs had not yet given the oath, but this changed very quickly, for no chief would put his people in danger. One after one, they came to the sheriffs and submitted to King William, to Dalrymple, until not a single clan opposed the government any longer.

Yet among the survivors was the baby boy Alexander, kept warm in his nurse's plaid, and it was he who represented our people during those days, fifty-three years later, when our hopes finally rose again.

Prince Charles Stuart, grandson of our King James, began the rebellion of 1745 by landing in the Isles in July. He was called Bonnie Prince Charlie, and his army grew throughout the summer, drawing many of the Gaels. The MacDonalds of Glen Coe were among the first to join him, marching behind a bunch of heather held aloft on a pike.

In short order, our army took Perth in the Highlands,

Linlithgow in the Lowlands, and soon Edinburgh itself, where Prince Charles was welcomed with the cheers of the crowds in the middle of September. He held court there, at Holyrood Palace, for several weeks. On the 21st of September, we met a government army at Prestonpans, near Edinburgh, and routed them. Our men watched redcoats run in fear, taking hundreds of them prisoner.

After securing the Lowlands, the Gaels marched into England, taking Carlisle and Manchester and coming as far south as Derby, a little over one hundred miles from London, in early December. Yet Prince Charles' war council decided to return to Scotland in order to regroup and bolster our forces. A government army followed from the south, led by King George's son William.

So it was that on the 16th of April, 1746, upon the moor of Culloden, the MacDonalds of Glen Coe lined up on the left flank with our swords and muskets. The Highlanders' bagpipes wailed, and the government's drums banged. After a short while, the government's artillery began their fire. They had 122 cannons, while the Gaels had only 12. The cannon fire picked off the clansmen, slowly, again and again, as we waited for the order to charge.

No order came from Prince Charles for thirty minutes, and when finally it did, the Highland men ran across the moor into massive cannon volleys, then short-range gunfire. As more clansmen fell, the remaining men tried to regroup, and then ran.

After the battle, government troops came into Highland towns and villages. They shot and bayoneted many. They burned houses and farms and took away livestock. Out of one hundred Glen Coe men who were of fighting age, fifty-two were killed during the rebellion.

The English now did all in their power to unravel us. Their government in London made it illegal for us to wear a kilt. They made it illegal for us to play the bagpipe. Their Parliament passed laws to prevent Gaelic children from being "educated in disaffected or rebellious principles." Since those days, our children often have been taught in English, learning about the Glorious Revolution of 1688, which brought the blessings of liberty to our United Kingdom.

Some of the departures, in those first few years, were men who had been captured at Culloden, or who had been arrested after the battle for their support of Prince Charles. So many were convicted in England and Edinburgh, and those who were not executed were forced onto ships bound for the West Indies and the American colonies. Too, there were the boys and young men who were sold into indentured servitude, and were shipped away from us, to the ports that served the tobacco trade.

The chief of Glen Coe, and all of the other chiefs, could do nothing, for the laws passed by the English had taken away their power. Our chiefs became mere landlords, with many of them moving to London. Clansmen and clanswomen have become mere tenants, with no claim to our own homes, and in the decades since Culloden, many of the Gaels have been forced from our lands.

I was a young boy when our men returned from Culloden, when the first of our people left, and I have seen many more go away since those times. I am old now, but I have stayed in the place where my mother and father are buried. I have stayed in the place where my memories lie.

There are the times when I hear that another one of our families is preparing to leave, and I wish I might say to them: Please do not go. Please do not leave. Remain here with us.

I wish I might say to them: There is yet a chance that we will come to our strength again, and give our last resistance. There is yet a chance that we will gain the freedom to keep to our ways.

But they speak only of green fields to the horizon, of the growing farms of Ohio and Virginia, of Ontario and the Carolinas. A man and woman might own hundreds of acres, they say, and leave wealth behind for their children. New machines await, with the spreading cities.

I bid them farewell, and as they go away from us, I pray they will always remember that they are the children of Mac-Iain, who should drink from the waters of the Coe. I pray they will remember our fathers, who fell so that we could remain here in our glen. I pray that our strength will remain in them, for all of their days, even while they are so far away across the sea.

They believe, and they say, that their grandchildren and great-grandchildren will know of us. They believe that the young ones will hold on to us.

Yet I know those young ones will not. They will sing only the songs of their new world, and every corner of their hearts will owe allegiance to their new country. They will speak only the language of the British Empire. They will never gaze upon the snowed peak of *Buachaille Etive Mòr* and know, in that moment, that they are at home.

With each generation, we will fade away from them, more and yet more. Then the time will arrive, some day, when they forget us at last.

CHAPTER 27

REUNION

The church bell in Glencoe was ringing as my family and I arrived. We stepped out of our cars, and saw the peaks of *Sgorr na Cìche* and *Sgorr nam Fiannaidh* above us in the distance, and then walked through the old door.

Here, sitting in the pews, were the descendants of the MacDonalds of Glencoe.

Here was Colin from New Zealand, descendant of Alasdair MacIain, who was just a few days late in giving the oath. Here was Lachie from the Isle of Lismore, the probable descendant of Angus MacDonald of Achnacon, who stood outside his house and escaped into the mountains by throwing his kilt over the heads of soldiers. Here was Brundage from Nova Scotia, descendant of another Angus MacDonald, whose children all departed for Canada.

Alistair from down the street was ill today, but his son Alexander was here. So were his wife Rosalin and her sister Jeanette, descendants of Duncan Rankin, who was the first one killed. There were so many others, too—cousins I was sure to meet soon.

We walked out after the service and gathered behind the bagpiper at the front of the church. The piper began to play, and we followed him, walking through the village and past the old bridge until we came to the memorial, a Celtic cross on a hill.

We stood together around it. Mountains were on all sides. The minute of silence began, and we bowed our heads and closed our eyes. In those first few seconds, the wind picked up a bit, then tapered off. Somebody was clearing his throat, somebody was whispering.

But I was thinking about her, the new one. She was just nine months old, daughter of my brother David and his wife Sarah. She was the first of the next generation, the first of Grandma and Grandpa's great-grandchildren, and I was thinking of her big eyes. I was thinking of her crib and her grin. And I was thinking of what I wanted to tell her right now:

You have breathing lungs, and a name.

You get to exist.

You are here, to have a beating heart, to squint at the sun. You are here to hear every note, to go running and grinning while your mom and dad chase after you. You are here to grow into new clothes, and then to go to the dance, and then to hold your diploma.

You are here to never back down, and to always let people in.

For you, too, there might come a time, one day, when the wrinkles are reconciled, and the shadows lengthen across the bedroom floor, and your little ones have little ones of their own, running into your arms. In those far off days, they'll climb around on you, and their eyes will look up into yours. Right then, for the first time ever, you might realize what it was like for your grandma to hold you in her arms so many years before, and watch over you.

And when these grandchildren of yours are a little older, they'll ask you about where they come from, and maybe this is when you'll sit back in your chair and pause. Maybe you'll smile, look away into the distance for a bit, and think about how to say it all. Then you'll begin to tell them about us.

Their ancestors.

Tell them our stories, and tell them what we used to say. Tell them about the ones who had to flee, and the ones who made a new life.

Tell them that our old hearts are still full.

Say that we never forgot the big things, and say that we always held fast, and say that we have left all of our traces behind.

Say that we are shining, for them, like stars in the darkened sky.

Notes and Acknowledgements

A portion of the proceeds from the sale of this book will go to the Glencoe Heritage Trust. To find out more, please go to www.glencoe-heritage-trust.com.

I would like to thank my wife Penny, and all of my family, for believing in this book and making it possible. I would also like to thank my cousins and friends who were central to this story and have graciously allowed me to recount their parts in it: Bob and Judy Collins, Elizabeth DiMichele, Namjoo and Armita Hashemi, Alistair and Rosalin MacDonald, Brundage and Ella MacDonald, Colin and Doreen MacDonald, Lachie and Diane MacDonald, Michael MacDonald, Alexander Mc-Donald, David McDonald, Jim McDonald, Leroy McDonald, and Robert and Jeanette Watt.

I am grateful for the help of the genealogists, researchers and others who provided the clues that led the way: Ray Bell, Anne Taylor Brown, Charles Hamble, Michael Hait, Dennis Korinek, Mark MacDonald, Kathy Vockery, James Ward, Harriett Worrell, and the archivists and other staff members at the Library of Virginia. I am thankful, as well, for the many people whose Internet pages and posts have shed light on this path, anonymously or not.

In addition, I appreciate Katherine Boyle's critiques and steadfast support, David Drummond's cover design, Stephanee Killen's editing, Erik Christopher's e-book conversion, and Snehal Avichal's website design. Thanks, also, to Michael Bauer for his Gaelic translations, to Jim McLean for permission to quote lyrics from his song "The Massacre of Glencoe," and to Andrew, Paul and Neil for getting Penny to the church on time.

Finally, please note that the spellings of certain words in older quotations have been modernized in the text, and that a pseudonym was used to protect the privacy of one person.

Source Notes

Note: The Massacre of Glencoe, and the broader history of the Scottish Highlands as sketched in this book, have been so well documented—and so often retold—that particular citations are unnecessary. However, all historical facts stated in the text, including all quotes from historical figures and documents, can be verified by consulting the sources listed in the Bibliography.

Chapter 1:

"Blow on a dead man's embers": Graves, Robert. *Complete Poems, Volume 2*. Manchester: Carcanet, 1997, 96.

Chapter 2:

"The Economist, *in a book review"*: "Big Macs." *The Economist* 15 June 2000.

"They came in a blizzard": McLean, Jim. "The Massacre of Glencoe." Duart Music, 1963.

Chapter 3:

"According to some websites, the name McDaniel": Hanks,

Patrick, ed. *Dictionary of American Family Names*. Vol. 2. New York: Oxford University Press, 2003.

Chapter 5:

"I am not, and never will be," etc.: Basu, Paul. *Highland Homecomings: Genealogy and Heritage Tourism in the Scottish Diaspora*. Abingdon, Oxfordshire: Routledge, 2007, 2, 177-78, 183.

Chapter 12:

The aspects of Highland culture sketched in this chapter, including the Gaelic proverbs and the story of Alasdair MacDonald of Keppoch, are set forth here: Newton, Michael. *Warriors of the Word: The World of the Scottish Highlanders*. Edinburgh: Birlinn, 2009.

Chapter 17:

"Alistair MacDonald is not a rich man," etc: MacWilliam, Bruce. "The MacDonalds of Glencoe." *Scots Heritage Magazine* Aug. 2003: 48-51.

Basu, Paul. *Highland Homecomings: Genealogy and Heritage Tourism in the Scottish Diaspora.* Abingdon, Oxfordshire: Routledge, 2007.

Beattie, William, ed. *Life and Letters of Thomas Campbell.* Vol. 1. London: Hall, Virtue & Co., 1852.

Boardman, Stephen. *The Campbells: 1250-1513.* Edinburgh: John Donald, 2006.

Buchan, John. *The Massacre of Glencoe.* 1933. Staplehurst, Kent: Spellmount, 1999.

Davis, Julia. *Never Say Die: The Glengarry McDonalds of Virginia.* Stafford, Virginia: American History Press, 1980.

Devine, T.M. *Clanship to Crofters' War: The Social Transformation of the Scottish Highlands.* Manchester: Manchester University Press, 1994.

— *Clearance and Improvement: Land, Power and People in Scotland 1700-1900.* Edinburgh: John Donald, 2006.

— *Scotland's Empire and the Shaping of the Americas 1600-1815.* Washington, D.C.: Smithsonian, 2003.

— *The Tobacco Lords: A Study of the Tobacco Merchants of Glasgow and Their Trading Activities c. 1740-90.* 1975. Edinburgh: Edinburgh University Press, 1990.

Devine, T.M., ed. *A Scottish Firm in Virginia 1767-1777.* Edinburgh: Scottish Historical Society, 1984.

Dobson, David. *Scottish Emigration to Colonial America, 1607-1785*. Athens, Georgia: University of Georgia Press, 2004.

Driscoll, Stephen. *Alba: The Gaelic Kingdom of Scotland AD 800-1124*. Edinburgh: Birlinn, 2002.

Drummond, John. *Memoirs of Sir Ewen Cameron of Locheill, Chief of the Clan Cameron*. Edinburgh: Maitland Club, 1842.

Duffy, Christopher. *The '45: Bonnie Prince Charlie and the Untold Story of the Jacobite Uprising*. London: Cassell, 2003.

"Big Macs." *The Economist* 15 June 2000.

Fairweather, Barbara. *Eilean Munda: The Burial Isle in Loch Leven*. Glencoe: Glencoe and North Lorn Folk Museum.

— *Glencoe: A Short History*. Glencoe: Glencoe and North Lorn Folk Museum, 2006.

Forbes, Robert. *The Lyon in Mourning*. 3 vols. Edinburgh: Scottish Historical Society, 1896.

Fyfe, J.G. *The Massacre of Glencoe*. Stirling, Scotland: Eneas MacKay, 1948.

Galenson, David. *White Servitude in Colonial America: An Economic Analysis*. Cambridge: Cambridge University Press, 1981.

Graves, Robert. *Complete Poems, Volume 2*. Eds. Beryl Graves and Dunstan Ward. Manchester: Carcanet, 1997.

Hanks, Patrick, ed. *Dictionary of American Family Names*. Vol. 2. New York: Oxford University Press, 2003.

Hopkins, Paul. *Glencoe and the End of the Highland War*. Edinburgh: John Donald, 1998.

Hunter, James. *A Dance Called America: The Scottish Highlands, the United States and Canada*. Edinburgh: Mainstream, 1995.

— *Glencoe and the Indians*. Edinburgh: Mainstream, 1996.

— *Last of the Free: A History of the Highlands and Islands of Scotland*. Edinburgh: Mainstream, 1999.

Linklater, Magnus. *Massacre: The Story of Glencoe*. London: Collins, 1982.

Martin, Martin. *A Description of the Western Islands of Scotland Circa 1695*. 1703. Edinburgh, Birlinn, 1999.

MacDonald, Angus and Archibald MacDonald. *The Clan Donald*. 3 vols. Inverness: Northern Counties, 1896-1904.

Macdonald, Donald J. *Clan Donald*. 1978. Gretna, Louisiana: Pelican, 2008.

— *Slaughter Under Trust: Glencoe 1692*. 1965. Greenville, Delaware: Delaware Free Press, 1982.

Macdonald, Iain S. *Glencoe and Beyond: The Sheep-Farming Years 1780-1830*. Edinburgh: Birlinn, 2005.

MacDonald, Norman H. *The Clan Ranald of Knoydart and Glengarry: A History of the MacDonalds or MacDonells of Glengarry*. 2nd ed. Edinburgh: Norman H. MacDonald, 1995.

MacWilliam, Bruce. "The MacDonalds of Glencoe." *Scots Heritage Magazine* Aug. 2003: 48-51.

Marsden, John. *Somerled and the Emergence of Gaelic Scotland*. 2000. Edinburgh: John Donald, 2008.

McDonald, Alexander. *The MacDonalds of Glencoe*. Glencoe: Alexander McDonald, 1998.

McDonald, Cornelia. *A Diary with Reminiscences of the War and Refugee Life in the Shenandoah Valley 1860-1865*. 1875. Nashville, Tennessee: Cullom & Ghertner, 1934.

McDonald, David. "Alexander Macdonald of Glencoe and the Forty-Five." *Clan Donald Magazine* 10 (1984.)

McDonald, David. *Clan Iain Abrach: A History of the MacDonalds of Glencoe*. Gamlingay, Cambridgeshire: Authors

OnLine, 2012.

McLean, Jim. "The Massacre of Glencoe." Duart Music, 1963.

Moffat, Alistair. *The Faded Map: Lost Kingdoms of Scotland*. Edinburgh: Birlinn, 2010.

Newton, Michael. *Warriors of the Word: The World of the Scottish Highlanders*. Edinburgh: Birlinn, 2009.

Plank, Geoffrey. *Rebellion and Savagery: The Jacobite Rising of 1745 and the British Empire*. Philadelphia: University of Pennsylvania Press, 2006.

Pollard, Tony, ed. *Culloden: The History and Archaeology of the Last Clan Battle*. Barnsley, South Yorkshire: Pen and Sword, 2009.

Prebble, John. *Culloden*. 1967. London: Penguin, 1996.

— *Glencoe*. 1966. London: Penguin, 1968.

— *The Highland Clearances*. 1963. London: Penguin, 1969.

Reid, Stuart. *The Scottish Jacobite Army 1745-46*. Botley, Oxfordshire: Osprey, 2006.

Richards, Eric. *The Highland Clearances*. 2000. Edinburgh: Birlinn, 2008.

Roberts, John L. *Clan, King and Covenant: History of the Highland Clans from the Civil War to the Glencoe Massacre*. Edinburgh: Edinburgh University Press, 2000.

— *Feuds, Forays and Rebellions: History of the Highland Clans 1475-1625*. Edinburgh: Edinburgh University Press, 1999.

Sadler, John. *Glencoe: The Infamous Massacre 1692*. Stroud, Gloucestershire: Amberley, 2010.

Scott, Walter. *The Waverley Anecdotes*. Vol. 1. London: J. Cochrane and J. McCrone, 1833.

Sellar, W.D.H. "The Earliest Campbells—Norman, Briton or Gael?" *Scottish Studies* 17 (1973): 109-126.

Simms, John Gerald. *War and Politics in Ireland, 1649-1730*. London: Hambledon, 1986.

Sykes, Bryan. *Adam's Curse: The Science That Reveals Our Genetic Destiny*. Norton: New York, 2004.

— *The Seven Daughters of Eve: The Science That Reveals Our Genetic Ancestry*. Norton: New York, 2001.

Thomson, Oliver. *The Great Feud: The Campbells and the MacDonalds*. Stroud, Gloucestershire: Sutton, 2000.

Williams, Flora McDonald. *The Glengarry McDonalds of Virginia*. Louisville, Kentucky: George G. Fetter, 1911.

About the Author

Ryan Littrell grew up in Chatham, Illinois and graduated from Northwestern University, followed by Boston College Law School, where he served as an Executive Editor of the *Boston College Law Review*. He lives in New York City, and *Reunion* is his first book.

To find out more, please go to www.RyanLittrell.com.

Made in the USA
San Bernardino, CA
28 September 2013